East of England

REAL·HERITAGE·PUBS

Pub Interiors of Special Historic Interest

EDITED BY
PAUL AINSWORTH AND
MICHAEL SLAUGHTER

T0386313

Based on CAMRA's East of England Regional Inventory of Historic Pub Interiors

Produced by CAMRA's Pub Heritage Group
www.heritagepubs.org.uk
info.pubheritage@camra.org.uk

For CAMRA Books
Managing Editor: Alan Murphy
Sales and Marketing: Toby Langdon

Book design/typography: Dale Tomlinson
Map: Igloo

Published by the Campaign for Real Ale Ltd
230 Hatfield Road, St Albans,
Hertfordshire AL1 4LW
www.camra.org.uk/books

© Campaign for Real Ale 2022

First Published 2022

ISBN 978-1-85249-381-3

A CIP catalogue record for this book is available
from the British Library

Printed and bound in the UK by Short Run Press Ltd, Exeter

This is the first pub heritage book to be published
since the untimely death of Dr **Geoff Brandwood**.
Geoff edited two books in this series (for the
South East and the North West) plus (with Jane
Jephcote) *London Heritage Pubs: An Inside Story*
and two editions of *Britain's Best Real Heritage
Pubs*. On top of that, his advice and guidance
was invaluable to those of us involved with other
books in the series. He is hugely missed.

PHOTO CREDITS
(Key: t=top; b=bottom; m=middle; l=left; r=right)

Photographs © Michael Slaughter LRPS apart
from the following:

Geoff Brandwood (p6br, p71t); Julian Calverley
(p72t); Stella Cattermole (p84br); Michael
Croxford (p 34t, bl, p87br, ml, p118br);
Andrew Davison (p77mr, bl, br); Derek Gibson
(p118bl, p119br); Tricia Halstead (p119ml, bl);
Lily Le Grice (p84tr); Andy Shaw (p42tr, p78t,
p111mr); JD Wetherspoon PLC (p117t, p118tl, tr).

Front cover: King's Head, Laxfield
Back cover: Crown Hotel, Downham Market

Contents

CAMRA and Pub Heritage

CAMRA was founded in 1971 to save Britain's traditional beer, but it soon became clear to campaigners that the best places to drink such beer, our pubs, were also under threat. In due course, CAMRA assigned equal importance to campaigning for real ale and for pubs.

The 1960s onwards saw a huge increase in the opening out of pubs and removals of fine fittings, so preservation of historic pub interiors emerged as a key campaigning issue. After pioneering work in York in the late 1980s, CAMRA set up a specialist Pub Preservation Group which evolved into today's Pub Heritage Group. The first step was to identify the most intact interiors surviving across the country's (then) 70,000 pubs. This massive task meant following up thousands of leads, developing criteria for inclusion, recording what was found (in words and photos) and creating a list – the National Inventory of Historic Pub Interiors. This initially focused on interiors still largely unaltered since before the Second World War, though intact early post-war pubs were later admitted. A further development was to include pubs with specific features or rooms of real national importance.

The first National Inventory was published in 1997 and totalled 179 entries. From then on, it was continually refined and updated as new candidates were discovered and, sadly, existing entries lost. Regional Inventories were the next step. As would be expected, the criteria for inclusion were set lower, though the same principles applied, with the emphasis on the internal fabric of the pub and what is authentically old. We later acknowledged a third category – pubs that had experienced still more change but which retained historic rooms or features felt to be of 'some regional interest'.

We have recently simplified the system by moving to a single listing within which interiors are graded as three, two or one star. The selection criteria are summarised on p18.

All these pubs can be found on our website, **pubheritage.camra.org.uk**, where clicking on the 'Search Here' facility will take you to easy-to-use drop-down menus.

Pubs to Cherish

East of England Real Heritage Pubs celebrates 76 pub interiors in Bedfordshire, Cambridgeshire, Essex, Hertfordshire, Norfolk and Suffolk which CAMRA has identified as having special historic interest. They represent an important aspect of the area's cultural and built heritage, with quite a number being true national treasures.

That said, they account for less than 2% or so of the pubs in the area. Why is this so? A major reason, of course, is that pub interiors have always been subject to change. The only pubs that are exactly the same as the day they opened are ones that came into being in the last few years. The pace of change, though, accelerated dramatically from the 1960s. At that time, a mania began for opening out, faddish theming, image change and general trashing. Consequently, many pubs suffered makeovers during which most, if not all, vestiges of original or early features were lost. Of the 90 pubs that featured in the first edition of this guide, ten have been ruined inside whilst another ten have closed altogether.

Recent years have seen a hugely welcome explosion in the number of micropubs. These intimate spaces are all about the time-honoured reason why many people visit a pub – 'good conversation and good beer'. It's all the more surprising, therefore, that some pub owners still want to remove walls and make rooms larger. There are many examples of pubs doing this then closing a year or so later.

The irony is that interest in historic buildings has never been greater. Lots of us are fascinated by our built heritage and spend time visiting historic buildings of many kinds. It is, though, only in recent years, and largely as a result of CAMRA's efforts, that pub interiors have come to be valued by mainstream conservationists. CAMRA picked up the baton on behalf of our pub heritage, filling the gaps in knowledge of what is out there, and actively seeking to protect what is left. It has worked closely with Historic England (formerly known as English Heritage) to gain statutory protection through the listing process for the most important examples we have identified.

CAMRA has now produced guides covering all regions of the country, but the early ones, like our first East Anglia guide (published in 2005), are now well out of date, hence this new edition. As with the other guides, it draws on many years of work by CAMRA members to track down and record those pub interiors that have escaped the attention of the modernisers and 'improvers'. Our photos will, we hope, testify to the historic importance of these pubs and encourage you to visit them. Their survival depends on being well-used, so you can do your bit whilst having great pub experiences at the same time.

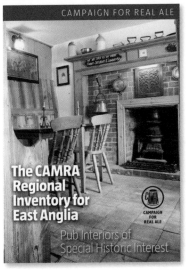

CAMPAIGN FOR REAL ALE

The CAMRA Regional Inventory for East Anglia

Pub Interiors of Special Historic Interest

CAMPAIGN FOR REAL ALE

What Shaped Pubs in the East of England?

Is there such a thing as a 'typical' East of England pub? Given the large and varied nature of the region and the fact that its pubs have taken shape over many years, the answer, essentially, is 'no'. By and large, pubs developed in much the same ways as in the rest of the country, though with no large cities, the region is bereft of the grand late-Victorian edifices which adorn the likes of London, Birmingham, Liverpool and Manchester. On the other hand, the area is blessed with many fine smaller pubs, both rural and urban, and a few are quite remarkable survivors. But first, a bit of history.

In the beginning

Most early public houses were literally just that – ordinary houses whose owners opened up a room or two to sell drink to neighbours. All you needed was somewhere to store the merchandise, somewhere to serve it and somewhere for customers to drink it. Pub keeping was a family business and, especially in the countryside, usually part-time, combined with, say, farming, carting, blacksmithing or some other trade. Such dual uses sometimes survived a long time – the Crown, in Snape, Suffolk (p113), for instance, had,

until as recently as 2019, a smallholding attached where the licensee kept goats and pigs. Nearly all these very homely pubs have gone now because such small businesses are no longer an economic proposition, and none survive in the East of England.

Several larger pubs do, however, occupy very old buildings and provide a glimpse of what pubs were like when they were places of relaxation for farm workers and others living in the immediate vicinity. Much of the King's Head, in Laxfield, Suffolk (p106), for instance, dates from the 16th century, and the servery in particular, with its absence of a bar counter, would be recognisable to drinkers from long ago. The Green Dragon,

King's Head, Laxfield

Green Dragon, Wymondham

Butt & Oyster, Pin Mill

in Wymondham, Norfolk (p92) is in an even older building, a 15th-century hall house and originally the hostelry to the nearby Benedictine monastery. The White Hart Hotel in St Albans (p69) part-occupies a late-15th-century range of timber-framed buildings. The core of the Butt & Oyster, in Pin Mill, Suffolk (p111) is 17th century and it isn't difficult to conjure up visions of its ancestral maritime (and smuggling) past.

Inns and taverns

The other types of establishment up until the early 19th century were the tavern and the inn. The former existed only in larger towns, catering for the more prosperous customer by serving wine and food. They were never common, and no former taverns still exist in East Anglia.

Inns provided meals and accommodation for better-off travellers, along with stabling for their horses, and many survive, albeit in vastly altered form. The Scole Inn, Norfolk (not included in this book) is probably the most impressive, and despite the internal ravages, still gives you a feel of what these places were like. More intact interiors can be found at the White Hart Hotel in St Albans – which claims to have had stabling for 50 horses in the 1750s – the Bull, in Long Melford, Suffolk (p110), and the Crown, in Downham Market, Norfolk (p78).

White Hart Hotel, St Albans

Bull, Long Melford

Crown Hotel, Downham Market

Both the Great North Road and the Old North Road passed through the east of the region with coaching inns every ten miles or so to allow changes of horses. Lots of these pubs survive and are externally impressive – e.g., the Bell, Stilton, and the George, Huntingdon, both in Cambridgeshire, and the White Hart, Welwyn, Hertfordshire – but the only one with an interior of sufficient historic interest for our purposes is the White Horse, in Eaton Socon, Cambridgeshire (p32).

White Horse, Eaton Socon

The Victorian pub

The pub as we know it today is mostly a Victorian creation. The first part of the 19th century saw the widespread adoption of counter service and the hand-pumped beer engine, heralding the change from an essentially domestic environment into a form of shop which could handle a greater volume of trade. Just as most rural pubs once catered primarily for the agricultural labourer, vast numbers of urban pubs were fairly basic establishments for the working man. In industrial areas especially, pubs afforded welcome refreshment after a shift down the pit, in the steelworks, or a day of hard labour. However, such industrialisation largely passed the East of England by so pubs of this kind always were few and far between. Some basic 'back street boozers' could once be found in places like Peterborough and Norwich, but these have now either been closed or gentrified. The Swan, in Bushey, Hertfordshire (p61), with its mid-terrace location, is perhaps the nearest we have to a place like this.

From early Victorian times, under the influence of social reformers and the Temperance lobby (see p77), a drive began to improve licensed premises and reduce their numbers. This encouraged the multi-room principle with its ability to offer a choice of 'better' rooms and thus attract a more respectable clientele. Most multi-roomed interiors have been opened up over the years, but in our towns and cities you can still find pubs of the era that retain plan-form and fittings from their early days. Particularly good examples are the Woolpack in Ipswich (p105), the Champion of the Thames in Cambridge (p31) and the Rose & Crown in Bury St Edmunds (p100). Rural pubs from this time still with a 19th-century ambience include the Walnut Tree, Broads Green, Essex (p46), the Blue Ball,

The Cock, Broom

Champion of the Thames, Cambridge

Walnut Tree, Broads Green

The years around 1900 proved to be the high point of pub-building and design, with grand, ornate 'palace' pubs arriving in bigger towns and cities, but also with lesser variants being built elsewhere. Sadly, the East of England mostly missed this aspect of the 'golden age'. The Painters Arms in Luton (p26), which is actually Edwardian, is the best example of the style with its wonderful tiling and surviving screenwork.

Grantchester, Cambridgeshire (p32), and the Bar/Parlour at the Queen's Head, Tolleshunt D'Arcy, Essex (p57). We must also mention here the Cock, in Broom, Bedfordshire, a mid-19th-century pub built without a bar counter, a configuration that continues to this day – there are only seven such pubs in the country and the East of England has two of them.

Plan of the Painters Arms, Luton

Between the wars

The Great War brought pub-building to a full stop, but it resumed quite soon afterwards. Pubs at first continued to be built on traditional lines, but before long we saw arrival of the 'improved' pub, often built for growing suburbs and busy highways. Reducing the number of pubs but improving standards in what remained had been the mission of magistrates for some years, and there was now a concerted drive to broaden the appeal of pubs and reduce their dependence on alcohol sales alone. The idea was for pubs to offer a 'respectable' environment with a range of rooms and facilities that encouraged civilised behaviour and patronage by the middle classes.

Brewers responded to these developments with a fresh surge of pub-building from the mid-1920s. Art Deco was the emblematic architectural style in this period but was adopted only rarely for pubs. The Nags Head, in Bishop's Stortford, Hertfordshire (below), exemplified the style superbly until quite recently and vestiges can still be seen, especially in the former public bar. The architect E. B. Musman also designed the iconic (but internally ruined) Comet at Hatfield.

Nags Head, Bishop Stortford

Also popular between the wars was a style sometimes called Tudor-bethan, or mock-Tudor, which sought to evoke the days of Merrie England. Externally, you'd find the likes of fake half-timbering, tall, mullioned windows and steeply pitched roofs with interiors featuring, perhaps, big 'Jacobean' staircases, large, ornate stone fireplaces, and heavily beamed ceilings. The Tudor Hall-style room in the Dunstable Arms, in Sheringham, Norfolk (p93), which is currently closed, is a fine example. The Rose & Crown, Rochford is a good example of a mock-Tudor exterior.

Dunstable Arms, Sheringham

Rose & Crown, Rochford

A notable development very much in this style was the construction around 1930 of several large 'road-houses' by the Tollemache (later Tolly Cobbold) brewery of Ipswich. With designs based on Helmingham Hall, the Tollemache family home, these huge structures, many with clock-towers and imposing chimney stacks, became known as 'Tolly Follies'. The Golden Hind in Ipswich (p101) is the least-altered survivor – an identical pub with the same name in Cambridge has undergone much more mauling. The Cricketers and Suffolk Punch in Ipswich, and the Golf Hotel in Rushmere are also still pubs, but inside all has changed. Others have been converted to housing or been demolished.

Golden Hind, Ipswich

Margaret Catchpole, Ipswich

The best surviving inter-war interior in the region, and arguably in the country, is the remarkable Margaret Catchpole, Ipswich (p104). Built by the local Cobbold brewery in 1936, it has its original plan-form, most of the contemporary fittings and even its bowling green. Despite being somewhat run-down at the time of writing, it really is the epitome of the 'improved' public house. Other pubs in the same style are the Gatehouse in Norwich (p86) and White Hart in Grays, Essex (p53).

White Hart, Grays

On a different scale, we have the Hand & Heart in Peterborough (p40), a largely untouched back-street local of 1938; the public bar, with its

Hand & Heart, Peterborough

distinctive 'Moderne' bar counter, is especially delightful.

Also of note are older pubs that were refitted between the wars in what was then up-to-date fashion. The Viper in Mill Green, Essex (p58), which is closed for refurbishment as this is written, is/was the best of these refits, with the Great Northern in Luton (p25) and Odd One Out in Colchester (p52) not far behind. The latter was a house until 1935 and retains the fittings from when it became a pub.

Post-war decline

Britain was bankrupt after the Second World War and hardly any pubs were built for a decade. When building restrictions were relaxed in 1954, new pubs began emerging again and were typified, unsurprisingly for these straightened times, by utilitarian design and low-quality materials. Layouts, though, still provided a choice of rooms, and such customary features as off-sales and concert rooms. Inevitably, once the economy picked up, these cut-price reminders of post-war austerity became highly unfashionable and few intact interiors from the period remain. However, difficult to love as they may be, they are important as reminders of how and where folk drank in those increasingly distant times.

The White Admiral of 1953 (p56) was the second pub built in Harlow New Town and has suffered surprisingly few alterations, with both public bar and saloon retaining most of their original fixtures and fittings. The Never Turn Back in Caister-on-Sea (not in this book), is a striking, Odeon-style beach-front extravaganza,

White Admiral, Harlow New Town

and there's just about enough left inside to give you a flavour of its 1957 origins.

Sadly, increased prosperity heralded a time of rapid and mostly regrettable change. The social divisions mirrored by the multi-roomed pub were vanishing, while magistrates and police favoured direct supervision of all parts of a pub from the serving area – hence the widespread removal of internal walls, to the great detriment of the atmosphere and attractiveness of most traditional pubs. Many pubs throughout the region were heavily influenced by their pub-owning brewery in the 1960s and 1970s, some being allowed to do their own thing, whilst others had to follow the company policy (if, indeed, they had one!) on how the pub interior was presented. In later years the corporate image became all important and is discernible today, even if done in a subtle way.

Having said that, some post-war refits of older pubs avoided the mania for trashing and now present a happily traditional appearance – both the Rose & Crown, Trowley Bottom, Hertfordshire (p70) and the Queen's Head, Newton, Cambridgeshire (p36), though significantly altered in post-war times, have achieved the 'timeless' atmosphere that many of us cherish. The Farriers Arms in St Albans (p68) and Cross Keys in Harpenden, Hertfordshire (p63), also very much look the part. On a smaller scale, this period saw the arrival of Formica bar tops – those at the Kings Arms, Blakeney, Norfolk (p75), in their original 'Watneys Red', are the best examples. The last

Wheel of Fortune, Alpington

remaining 'Watneys' 1960s bar-back fittings can be found at the Wheel of Fortune, Alpington (p75). Eccentric bar counters were also popular for a time, perhaps made from barrels (Crown Hotel, Downham Market, Norfolk [p78]) or with bottles inserted (Queen's Head, Newton [p36], and Crown, Houghton Regis, Bedfordshire [p24]).

Crown, Downham Market

At this time, a series of brewery mergers brought the majority of pubs into the ownership of one or other of the 'Big Six' national brewing conglomerates. All of these, in thrall to their corporate accountants and marketing men, inflicted huge damage on the pub heritage they inherited. Smaller brewers and many private owners shared this obsession to modernise.

There was no respite. The rise of off-licences, shops and supermarkets made pub off-sales redundant (see p102). Environmental health officers demanded changes to accommodate inside toilets and better food preparation

Cross Keys, Harpenden

Kings Arms, Blakeney

Queen's Head, Newton

to be viable. Happily, some have successfully met this challenge by extending their building in ways which don't impact adversely on their historic core. The Cock, Broom, Bedfordshire (p23) comprised, until fairly recently, just the two front rooms, but the expansion at the rear has been sensitively handled. The Three Horsehoes, Warham All Saints, Norfolk (p119), is also a cleverly managed blend of old and new.

Cock, Broom

Three Horsehoes, Warham All Saints, Norfolk

facilities. Old bar-back fittings were hacked about to make space for more varied products like wine, spirits and refrigerated drinks. Fire officers insisted on adaptations to provide safer escape routes. Such relentless pressures resulted in a much-depleted pub heritage.

The aftermath

Recent years have seen a sad decline in the overall numbers of traditional pubs in this country – down from around 70,000 in 1980 to 47,500 today. To some extent, this has been offset by an increase in bars, nearly all in town and city centres, but, with a few honourable exceptions, few have much merit in design terms. Some new pubs continue to be built, mostly 'family' pubs on the edges of towns, but conversions from other uses like banks and shops are much more common. However, some really good work can be found, and we celebrate outstanding conversions and restorations in this book.

Mentioned earlier were the particular pressures on small, rural pubs which struggle

Public interest in our built heritage has never been higher and the existence of this very book, published by CAMRA, and the popularity of others like it shows that this interest extends to our pubs as well. The article on p14 examines the threats our historic pubs face and what we can do about them.

Pubs in Peril

Since the first edition of this guide in 2005, pub numbers across the UK have fallen by some 11,000, representing 23% of the nation's pub stock. Many reasons can be identified for this gloomy state of affairs, including changing social habits, the effect of recent recessions, the widening differential between the prices of drinks bought at a pub and in a supermarket, the rapacious behaviour of many pub-owning companies, and the smoking ban. Over the past two years the COVID pandemic has inevitably hit many pub businesses very hard. A particular threat is the attractiveness of many pub buildings to developers. Conversion of rural pubs to houses has been all too common for many years but it's now our urban pubs that are really suffering. Many suburban pubs, for instance, occupy large plots of land, ideal for small supermarkets or similar developments, and in recent years hundreds have been lost in this way.

Such losses had been exacerbated by feeble planning laws that allowed the demolition of pubs and many changes of use without the need for planning permission. Strong campaigning by CAMRA and others led to these 'permitted development' rights being withdrawn in England in 2017, and despite the impact of the pandemic on trade, the closure rate has slowed down noticeably since.

This combination of negative factors has posed major problems for heritage pubs, especially urban ones. Many of the latter are to be found in unfashionable, off-centre locations where they have ticked along for many years, serving the local community. As a result, their owners saw little point investing in the kinds of major changes inflicted, in the pursuit of fashion, on many town or city centre pubs, so heritage was preserved, more or less by accident.

Sadly, though, when the recent recessions began to bite, these pubs tended to fall on the wrong side of the profit line.

Several pubs which would have met the criteria for this guide are currently under severe threat. The Cabinet, Reed, Hertfordshire, a fine old weatherboarded village pub, for instance, is the subject of a long-running planning dispute with owners who illegally converted it to a house in 2016, later opening part of it (again without planning permission) as a restaurant. A group of villagers is fighting to have it restored as a pub.

Greyhound, Flempton

The Greyhound in Flempton, Suffolk, has been closed an equally long time. Although a very old building, the chief heritage interest derives from a complete refit around 1960, most of which survives. We gather it has recently been sold, so it's one to watch. Closed since 2016, the Swan in Worlingworth, Suffolk has survived a plan for conversion into residential, It reopened as we

Swan, Worlingworth

were going to press but press photos indicate a loss of bar fittings. The Tower Arms in South Weald, Essex, occupying a stately former shooting lodge, has been shut even longer, though rumours of conversion to a high-end restaurant continue to circulate.

Other pubs of heritage importance have, sadly, gone altogether. The Palomino in Newmarket, Suffolk was an especially sad loss – a virtually intact (and therefore very rare) estate pub from 1963 that had been very close to being statutorily listed by Historic England in connection with a study of post-war pubs. It was demolished in 2020 and the site redeveloped for housing. The

Palomino, Newmarket

same fate befell the mighty Woodside, Thorpe St Andrew, Norwich – a post-war pub that had retained its original plan-form and impressed by its sheer scale. At the other end of the spectrum, several smaller, rural pubs with heritage interest have been converted to houses, with their urban equivalents generally becoming shops or restaurants.

Woodside housing estate, Thorpe St Andrew, Norwich

It isn't all doom and gloom, though. The Viper, Mill Green, Essex (p58), for instance, had become very dilapidated before closing altogether in 2019. Residential conversion seemed a likely fate, but new owners stepped in who are presently carrying out a major refurbishment which, we are assured, will fully respect all the historic features

Viper, Mill Green, Essex

in the listed building. When Greene King put the Lord Nelson in Burnham Thorpe, Norfolk (p76), up for sale, it was bought by Holkham Estates. They carried out a good refurbishment which included creating a replica of one of the two ancient, high-backed settles in the historic Nelson's Bar which had been removed in 2002. The wonderful King's Head, Laxfield, Suffolk (p106), had suffered the indignity of much of its superb panelling being painted in gastro shades,

Lord Nelson, Burnham Thorpe

but this was painstakingly removed by the community group who bought the pub in 2018 (see article on p72). Many non-heritage pubs have also been similarly rescued – a good example being the Suffield Arms in Thorpe Market, Norfolk, where a closed pub has been reopened by the owners of the nearby Gunton Arms (p119) as an 'overflow'. Like that pub, it's filled with artwork the owners have collected, some of which is, shall we say, challenging.

CAMRA's Pub Heritage Group will always fight to save historic pubs in peril. One tactic is to draw a threatened pub to the attention of an enlightened small pub company, and several pubs elsewhere in the country have been saved in just this way. We also get pubs statutorily listed – see the article about listing on p16. Where we can, we use the planning system to resist unwanted changes to heritage pubs and encourage local folk to do likewise. Most of all, we aim to generate interest in these precious survivors. Pubs are businesses and the more people use them, the less likely are they to wither and die.

You can do your bit by putting this guide to active use

Statutory Listing

All parts of the United Kingdom have systems for protecting buildings of special architectural or historic interest: 50 of the 76 pubs in this guide are statutorily listed. The process is devised not to *prevent* change but to *manage* it effectively, working with the grain of the building, not against it.

In England, listings are made by the Secretary of State for Culture, Media and Sport, on the advice of Historic England. There are three grades:

Grade I This highest grade covers the top 2.5% of all listed buildings; those described as having 'exceptional', even international interest. They include our cathedrals, most of our medieval churches, great public buildings, and major secular buildings of great antiquity. Three pubs/hotels in the East of England are listed at Grade I, but they do not feature in this guide as they contain few historic internal fittings: they are the Old Bell & Steelyard, Woodbridge, Suffolk; Scole Inn, Scole, Diss, Norfolk; and Red Lion Hotel, Colchester, Essex (see the article on page xx for more information about them). February 2020 saw the first Grade I listing of a Victorian pub, the magnificent Philharmonic Dining Rooms in Liverpool of *c*.1898; this resulted from a CAMRA-inspired initiative to Historic England to improve list descriptions for key pubs on the National Inventory of Historic Pub Interiors (see below).

Grade II* (spoken of as two star) This covers a further 5.5% of listed buildings which are deemed to have 'outstanding interest'. The Margaret Catchpole, Ipswich (p104), is one of very few inter-war pubs to be so highly graded. Other Grade II* pubs featured in this guide are the Green Dragon, Wymondham (p92), and the White Hart Hotel, St Albans (p69). The high grading of these two pubs is primarily due to the antiquity of their built fabrics, but their historic pub interiors simply enhance their claims to the high grade. Two more Grade II*-listed pubs are the Lattice House, King's Lynn, Norfolk, and St Peter's Hall, St Peter South Elmham, Suffolk, featured in the Heritage Pubs of the Future article (see page 116).

Grade II 92% of listed buildings fall into this category and have what is considered to be 'special historic interest.

CAMRA's Pub Heritage Group has successfully submitted applications for the statutory listing of many pubs with historic interiors. In the East of England these include the Painters Arms, Luton (1998); Margaret Catchpole, Ipswich at II* (1995); and the Viper, Mill Green (2019).

Margaret Catchpole, Ipswich

Historic England Projects to List More Pubs

Some years ago, Historic England identified public houses as the building type most at risk, and in 2013 embarked on a project to identify pubs built in the inter-war years that were worthy of statutory listing. They sought the assistance of Pub Heritage Group to identify potential candidates. This resulted in the listing at Grade II of 21 pubs, including two featured in this guide – Gate House, Norwich (p86) and White Hart, Grays (p53).

Gate House, Norwich

In 2015 Historic England embarked on a post-war pubs project and in 2018 five pubs were listed at Grade II which included the Never Turn Back, Caister-on-Sea (p11).

Historic England Project to Enhance Listed Descriptions of Pub Interiors

There is a common misconception that only particular features of a building will be listed. In fact, a listing covers the *entire* building, both inside and out, including its fixtures and fittings. Any changes (beyond normal care and maintenance) are unlawful unless 'listed building consent' has been obtained. Owners face unlimited fines and a possible order for reinstatement if unauthorised works are carried out. Even if a particular historic feature is not actually mentioned in the official list description it is still protected. This is vitally important since many older descriptions are not detailed and, in the case of pubs, the interior may not be mentioned at all.

Owners seeking change may try to persuade local authorities that this absence means something is not important. Although in law, the protection is there, local authorities may be unaware of the significance of a pub interior and be talked into granting permission.

Pub Heritage Group has campaigned successfully over the years with Historic England for improved list descriptions. This culminated in February 2020 in splendidly detailed descriptions for ten of our most precious pubs with historic interiors. The pubs were nominated by Pub Heritage Group and we were delighted with the announcement of the Grade I listing of Liverpool's Philharmonic Dining Rooms. A further ten pubs now have detailed descriptions reflecting the importance of their interiors as a result of the second round of this project, including the King's Head, Laxfield (p106).

King's Head, Laxfield

The Selection Criteria

Our listings of historic pub interiors focus entirely on the **internal physical fabric** of pubs and what is **authentically old** inside them.

Age

Interiors are eligible for consideration if they have remained essentially unaltered for at least the last 50 years.

General Principles

When assessing candidates, we look firstly at two key aspects:

- **Layout** – survival of historic layout and internal divisions, either intact or readily discernible;

- **Fittings & Decor** – items of particular interest include old or original bar counters, bar-backs, fixed seating, panelling and other joinery, plasterwork, ceramics and decorative glass.

They will be then judged against the following qualities:

- **Distinctiveness and Rarity** Interiors are likely to qualify if they are of special architectural importance and, in overall terms, of an interesting, distinctive and historically important nature. Fittings which may genuinely be old, but are banal and commonplace, are likely to be given lower markings. Rarity of survivals is also taken into account. Some types of historic interior are now (or always have been) scarce.

- **Impressiveness** Some interiors are immediately impressive because of the impact of a surviving style or design, or the quality of the fittings and fixtures. Weight is given to the general impression that an interior makes on an informed visitor.

- **Authenticity** Importance is placed on verifying from documentary or photographic sources where possible, the genuineness of supposedly historic internal fabric.

The Rankings

All entries stand out as being of particular national heritage interest, but there are inevitably notable variations in terms of intactness and quality, hence the ranking system we have adopted.

Three-star pubs have stayed wholly or largely intact for the last 50 years, or retain particular rooms or features that are truly rare or exceptional, or display a combination of the two.

Two-star pubs have interiors where the intactness and quality levels will be somewhat lower than for Three Star.

The interiors of **One-star** pubs will have either readily identifiable historic layouts or retain rooms or features of special interest, but more significant changes are allowable.

Conclusion

Our aim with the pub descriptions in this guide is to provide you with a good understanding of the historic significance of each of the pubs. Three-star pubs are, we believe, well worth going out of your way to make a special visit, whilst a detour to check out a Two-star pub would be time well spent, but we hope you will find visits to all the featured pubs an enjoyable and worthwhile experience.

Using this Guide

The descriptions in this guide make clear the significance of each pub interior. The entries fall into three categories:

★★★ CAMRA Three-star Real Heritage Pub is one that has stayed wholly or largely intact for the last 50 years, or retains a particular room or feature that is truly rare or exceptional, or displays a combination of the two.

★★ CAMRA Two-star Real Heritage Pub is one with an interior where the intactness and quality levels will be somewhat lower than for three star.

★ CAMRA One-star Real Heritage Pub one which has either a readily identifiable historic layout or retains rooms or features of special interest but is more changed than a three- or two-star pub.

The detailed selection criteria for the Inventories are set out on page 18 (opposite).

Real ale: at least one real ale on offer

Real cider: at least one real draught cider on offer

Meals lunchtime/evening: food available. This may vary from snacks such as rolls or pies to high-quality meals. We indicate the days/sessions we were advised when the book went to press. However, serving times can vary so please ring the pub ahead of a visit if you want food.

Regional map: on pages 128/inside back cover shows the location of all pubs listed in the guide.

Opening Hours

Opening times can vary considerably and can change. Where opening hours are restricted, the guide attempts to indicate what these are.

Prior to Lockdown we would have no hesitation in recommending CAMRA WhatPub https://whatpub.com as a reliable source of opening hours details. However, many pubs are still adjusting their hours of operating since Lockdown to match the likely trade, and it is very difficult to keep track of the changes licensees are making.

In the experience of the editors, pubs tend to keep their Facebook pages up to date for opening hours and phone numbers. We have therefore included a note of a pub's Facebook page, where they have one, in their entry.

If you are planning to make a visit to a pub at a particular time then we strongly recommend you ring the pub to check opening hours, particularly if likely to want a meal. You can also enquire about the real ale(s) that are likely to be on the bar.

Since Lockdown there has been a notable increase in the number of pubs closing earlier than their advertised hours 'as there were so few customers'. Again, we encourage users of the guide to contact a pub by phone or Facebook Messenger to ask for closing times.

Cautionary Words

This guide is concerned only with the internal fabric of pubs – not with qualities of atmosphere and welcome or even the availability of real ale. Inclusion is solely for a pub's physical attributes and should not be construed as a recommendation in any other sense.

On the Tiles

Over the years, pub designers have employed the use of ceramics in various forms, ranging from their mundane but very necessary use in toilets, through plain floor and wall tiles to ornate tiled dados and pictorial panels. Ceramic bar counters could also be found though few now survive and none in the East of England.

Two pubs in Luton hold particular delights for tile-lovers. The Great Northern (p25) makes up in character what it lacks in size and the dark-green-tiled dado panelling all round the room is especially attractive; it features, at regular intervals, a tall tulip-inspired relief in the Art Nouveau style. More plentiful tiling can be found nearby at the Painters Arms (p26). The main entrance lobby has a colourful patterned tiled floor as does the lobby for the now-disused entrance on the left in High Town Road – this also has wall tiling to half-height in shades of brown, topped off with an ornamental frieze featuring ferns and scallop shells. The same wall tiling appears in various places elsewhere in the interior, and at the rear of the public bar is a glazed, brown brick fireplace. Of particular note are two small tiled pictorial panels on the fireplace in the rear left area – one depicting a village pond with ducks enjoying themselves and the other sheep in a field with a strange, high-roofed building behind. The ground floor of the exterior is of green-glazed brick.

Sadly, the best tiled panel in the region isn't presently viewable. It's in the former entrance lobby at the Cliff, Hamlet Road, Southend (too altered for inclusion in this book) but is covered up for protection. The tiling is floor-to-ceiling and the multi-tile panel at the centre depicts a farm-girl with a pail against a background of farm buildings and a few cows. It is signed 'L. Hall 1888'. This pub, incidentally, also features a superb collection of Victorian back-painted mirrors behind the bar but they are, unfortunately, largely obscured by modern clutter.

The best tiled floor we have found is at the Red Lion Hotel, Cromer, Norfolk (p78) and separates the

The Painters, above and below

left-hand room from the dining area. It's Victorian in age and if not actually Minton then certainly in that style.

The White Hart, Grays (p53) has a passage whose dado is clad in brown inter-war tiling, while at the Rose & Crown, Rochford (p57), there's a dado of dark-brown glazed bricks in the gents'.

The Great Northern

The Cliff, Southend

Bedfordshire

BROOM

Cock ★★★

This splendid village local is one of only seven pubs in England that retain their historic total lack of a bar counter or hatch (the King's Head, Laxfield, Suffolk (p106) is another). It occupies a mid-19th-century row of cottages converted into an alehouse, then a pub, and is characteristic of the way thousands of village pubs may have begun, with just one small room in a private house, then expanding over the years. In this case, the original drinking area was to the left of the front entrance; it is now a games room. Drinks were fetched, as, amazingly, they still are, from the top of the cellar steps in the room beyond.

The right-hand front room

The right-hand front room was once a shop, hence the cupboards either side of the fireplace. It has plenty of panelling, full height on the rear wall and two-thirds height elsewhere. The entrance corridor also sports a highly decorative display of woodwork – old, lapped boarding on the right and further back a set of cupboards. The panelling on the left, however, is more recent, being the work of a local carpenter, Richard Beasley, in c.1980.

The snug

The uneven, red-tiled corridor leads to the rear part where, on the right, a small snug has been brought into use in modern times. It has a red-tiled floor, panelled walls, bench seating and an early-20th-century fireplace. Changes were made just outside this room in 1977 when the sink used for cleaning glasses was removed.

Further changes in the 1990s brought the toilets inside and also created a public drinking area in front of the entrance to the cellar servery. This has greatly expanded the pub's trading area but has not destroyed the atmosphere of the old front rooms. At the rear left is a dining room brought into use in the 1990s.

Closes at 7pm Sun.   23 High Street, SG18 9NA · 01767 314411
 The-Cock-at-Broom ; Listed Grade II; Planning: Central Beds
Real ale; Real draught cider; Meals lunch & evening (not Sun eve).

HOUGHTON REGIS

Crown ★

A thatched 17th-century pub retaining elements of a 1930s refit. Head firstly for the public bar which can only be accessed from its own exterior door, an increasingly rare phenomenon in today's pubs. This little-altered room has a parquet floor, panelled ceiling on the left and a full-height baffle/draught screen by the door. Also dating from the refit are the curved counter and the upper part of the bar-back with mirrored back and good columns holding up the shelves. Curved bench seating is attached to the dado panelling around the bay window with more either side of the counter: also, a brick fireplace painted cream and 'Gentlemen' sign on the door which both look to be inter-war. The lounge has an interesting ceiling and a brick fireplace, whose inlaying with bottles suggests a 1950s/60s date, but the bar fittings are modern. The only item of interest in the rear games room is the hatch for service.

East End, LU5 5LB · 01582 864457
TheCrownHoughton; Listed Grade II;
Planning: Central Beds; No Real Ale; No food.

Public bar (right-hand room)

LUTON

Great Northern ★★

The term 'little gem' has become something of a cliché, but springs immediately to mind on entering this tiny, one-bar pub. You enter by the left-hand door, which originally led to an off-sales, but the partition was removed many years ago and the former main entrance, the right-hand door, was put out of use. Green-tiled wainscotting with a tulip relief adorns all the walls and the ornate, cast-iron roof pillar with a leaf decoration is a notable feature. The mirrored bar-back, with slender columns holding up the shelves, is genuinely old; commendably, no lower shelves have been lost as the fridge is sensibly placed under the bar counter. This has a canted front painted turquoise, and like the brick fireplace is inter-war. The domino table at the front of the room, with holders for your pint glass in each corner, is a rare feature. Most of the external patterned glass has been replaced, presumably because of breakages, but all the original glazing bars (some curved) survive. At the back of the room is an exterior-looking etched window, beyond which was formerly a lounge but is now a smoking area.

63 Bute Street, LU1 2EY · 01582 729311
 The-Great-Northern-Luton; Planning: Luton;
Not listed; Real Ale; No food.

LUTON

Painters Arms ★★

Public bar

Rebuilt in 1913 with an interesting, green-glazed brick frontage, the Painters retains much superb internal tiling while its original compartment-alised layout is still easily discernible (see plan on page 9). The rare jug bar and the rest of the historic interior were saved in 1998 thanks to swift action by CAMRA and English Heritage (as was) to get the pub listed.

On entering, the small central entrance lobby has a patterned tiled floor. Ahead of you is a small snug created by two three-quarter-height partition walls with 'Jug Bar' etched in the door glass, indicating its original function as an off-sales. Sadly, the seats running down each side – no doubt used by customers having a swift one before leaving with their takeaways – have been removed in recent years. On the right, the public bar has its original bar fittings, but the counter-front and part of the bar-back have been painted a deep blue. At the rear is a glazed, brown-brick fireplace, and on either side the dado has tiles topped off with a brown and green frieze ornamented with ferns and scallop shells. The fixed seating is original.

To the left, two small rooms were amalgamated many years ago, but you can still see 'Saloon' and 'Private Bar' etched in the door window glass. The combined room retains an attractively tiled dado plus two original fireplaces, one including pictorial, green-tiled panels. The pot shelf is a relatively modern addition, but carefully created to include Art Nouveau-style glazing, harmonising with that in the original partitions. A wall at the back was removed in 2000 and a door widened, so now it is possible to circumnavigate the interior.

79 High Town Road, LU2 0BW · 01582 732815
 thepaintersarmsluton; Planning: Luton; Listed Grade II; Real Ale; No food.

Left-hand bar

TOTTERNHOE

Cross Keys ★

A 17th-century timber-framed thatched pub with two small bars that was last refurbished in the 1950s. In the small left-hand bar are a 1950s-style counter and a bar-back mixing 1950s and more recent work. The beams are replacements following a fire in 2004, hence why the insurance company prohibits use of the old fireplace. The tiled floor looks to be post-war. Through an opening (door removed), another small bar has an old quarry-tiled floor and a 1950s counter with a recent wood top replacement of a copper one. The very old brick-and-stone fireplace is now out of use and contains a table. Period doors lead to the ladies', gents' and cellar, the latter being notably low. The bar counters have recently been painted cream.

Mon–Thu 12–3pm, 5–11pm.
201 Castle Hill Road, LU6 2DA · 01523 220434
 crosskeystotternhoe; Listed Grade II; Planning: Central Beds; Real Ale; Meals Lunch & Evening Tue–Sat, lunch Sun.

Left-hand bar

Right-hand bar

Old Farm Inn ★

Formerly a farm building, most of what you now see dates from the 1950s when the extension on the right was added and the front bar extended into a former living room. This bar retains fittings from the time of the alterations, notably the counter and bar-back; some of the panelling and the inglenook fireplace are much older. There's an even better inglenook fireplace, with a copper hood, in the back lounge. The small counter, now painted black, is also from the 1950s, though the bar-back combines old and new. The presence of another fireplace at the back indicates that this space was once two rooms.

Mon–Thu 12–3pm, 5–11pm.
16 Church Road, LU6 1RE · 01582 670453
 oldfarminntotternhoe; Listed Grade II; Planning: Central Beds; Real Ale; Meals Lunch & Evening (not Sun eve).

Front bar

Back lounge

A Bite (or More) to Eat

Way back when, pubs were places to drink. The exceptions were inns and taverns, which mainly catered for travellers and therefore offered meals as well as drinks and a bed for the night. However, by the 19th century, even beerhouses often sold simple fare like bread and cheese or pork pies. It wasn't until the inter-war years, though, that food provision started to become important to the pub trade. The 'improved' public houses, favoured by licensing justices, promised a 'respectable' environment that would include food, invariably in designated rooms.

Many wet-led pubs also provided sustenance, albeit on a much more modest scale. George Orwell's 'ideal' back-street local, the Moon Under Water, for instance, had a snack counter selling liver-sausage sandwiches and mussels. By the 1960s, rolls or sandwiches (inevitably Cheese & Onion or Ham) might appear at lunchtimes until they ran out. Elsewhere, heated alternatives like pies and pasties could be available, kept in hot-food display cabinets, a few of which survive on bar tops. A common sight in the evenings, even until the 1980s, was the seafood salesman, visiting pubs with his wicker basket.

All pubs had snacks of some kind. Crisps first appeared in the 1930s, and by 1934 the largest producer, Smiths, boasted of supplying every pub in the country. The sachet of salt in every packet was a key ingredient as it made you thirsty! A jar of pickled eggs became a common sight on bar-backs. Salted peanuts came along in the 1950s while pork scratchings became popular from the 1970s.

menu

Prices include french fried potatoes, mushrooms, tomato, watercress, and roll and butter – plus ice cream or biscuits and cheese.

PRIME FILLET STEAK	approx 16/6
PRIME RUMP STEAK	approx 13/9
PRIME SIRLOIN STEAK	approx 13/3

All steaks are juicy prime beef and weigh about half a pound before cooking.

GOLDEN FRIED DOVER SOLE . approx **14/–**
(12 oz. approx. uncooked weight), with tartare sauce, lemon, watercress, french fried potatoes, roll and butter – plus ice cream or biscuits and cheese.

Berni's celebrated sherries from the wood in large glass or schooner.

This Berni Guide to Good Eating is one of a set of four, covering the entire country.

The food-oriented pub is very much a post-war creation, with increasing prosperity making eating out a part of family life. Berni Inns was founded in 1955 and had 147 outlets by 1970, many in what are now pubs. It was around this time that the Ploughman's Lunch emerged – nothing to do with actual ploughmen but dreamed up by an Ad-man on behalf of the British Cheese Board. 'Pub Grub' had arrived.

Meanwhile, the big brewers saw food as a money-spinner – it accounted for 9% of turnover in 1977 but double that by 1983. Chains emerged, starting with Beefeater in 1974, followed by Harvester, Brewer's Fayre, Hungry Horse, Toby Carvery, Table Table and many other family-oriented brands.

At the other end of the market, the gastropub was first sighted in London with the reinvention of a boozer called the Eagle in Farringdon as a gourmand's delight in informal surroundings. They are now commonplace and provoke mixed feelings among lovers of traditional pubs. On the one hand, anything that breathes new life into tired, old businesses is good. On the other, it seems compulsory to adopt the same, basic decorative scheme, slapping blue-grey or other pastel shades over all available woodwork in an effort to appear modern.

Many, if not most, of the pubs in this book serve food and it's generally a good thing, not least because the majority of rural pubs, in particular, wouldn't survive without it. Sometimes, especially when all tables are set for diners, the restaurant dimension overwhelms the pub one, but it's perfectly possible to provide good food without adversely affecting the traditional ambience of a pub, and you will find plenty of successful examples here.

Cambridgeshire

CAMBRIDGE

Champion of the Thames ★★

One of the last remaining traditional pubs in the city centre, the 'Champ' retains, largely unaltered, its late-19th-century interior. On entering, you will find a draft screen then a rare part-glazed partition wall separating the public bar on the left and the lounge on the right. A now-disused door, rear left, has an etched 'Public Bar' panel, indicating that a partition has been lost – the front door perhaps once accessed an off-sales.

The bare-boarded, wood-panelled public bar has a marvellous etched window, showing the Champion in action, but is not original, having been smashed and replaced several times (the pub lies on the notorious 'King Street Run'). It retains a Victorian panelled counter that was moved forward slightly in recent years. The bar-back looks mainly Victorian, though until the 1980s casks were stillaged in the lower portion; the mirrors are probably also modern. Old fitted seating survives at the front with a bare bench rear left.

The lounge (right-hand room)

The lounge, also panelled, and with a wood-block floor and another fine etched window, has a small, angled Victorian counter in the same style as that in the public bar. The small alcove once contained cupboards. At the front and attached to the partition are fixed benches with modern leather upholstery.

A passageway at the back leads to toilets added in the 1980s to replace rudimentary outside loos.

Opens at 4pm Sun–Thu. 68 King Street, CB1 1LN · 01223 351464
 ChampionOfTheThames; Listed Grade II; Planning: Cambridge; Real ale; No food;

Public bar (left-hand room)

EATON SOCON

White Horse ★

An early-18th-century coaching inn on the Great North Road. The oldest fittings are on the right-hand side and include a splendid fitted, curved, high-backed settle, a part-glazed partition wall, and another curved one at the rear of the servery. The wood surround of the inglenook fireplace and sections of dado panelling appear old. The layout of four small rooms across the front of the building has been like this for over 50 years, although it is unlikely that they were all bars in the past. The counters may be 1950/1960s but the bar-back shelves are modern. The area behind the bar on the left has seen recent changes and the building has been extended to the rear.

Closed Mon (not bank holiday) & Tue, opens at 4pm Wed.
103 Great North Road, PE19 8EL · 01480 470853;
 thewhitehorse.eatonsocon; Listed Grade II; Planning: Hunts;
Real Ale; Meals Lunch & Evening Thu–Sat, Wed eve, Sun lunch.

GRANTCHESTER

Blue Ball Inn ★★

The Blue Ball (whose name commemorates a balloon flight) is a small village local that dates from 1767 and was rebuilt in 1893. It is situated in the middle of a row of houses on a narrow road so you may need to park nearer the village centre. Purchased from a pub company by long-term regulars in 2014 to secure its future, it now offers food, accommodation, and also live music on a Thursday night. It retains its original two-bar layout and another room has been added recently.

The front door leads into the very small bar on the right with a bare wood floor, a bar counter that appears to be of pre-war date, a dado of heavy-duty wallpaper that looks like wood panelling, and fixed wood-backed bench seating. A step down on the left is the small main bar with a par-

Right-hand bar

Left-hand bar

LITTLE GRANSDEN

Chequers ★

A village pub with three small rooms that has been in the same family since 1951. Rebuilt after a fire in the late 19th century, it originally consisted of the two left-hand rooms with the right room added in the rebuild. Up to around 1960, the left-hand room contained a bar counter in the front right-hand part – markings on the ceiling and wall confirm this. It has a cracking, little public bar in the middle with a red-and-black quarry-tiled floor, old dado panelling and basic bare bench seating, the counter being added in the 1960s. It has a brick and wood surround fireplace at least 70 years old with a log fire. The right-hand room also has old dado panelling and a 1970s fireplace; the bar counter was added in the 1960s and has a modern frontage.

Closed Mon–Wed.   71 Main Road, SG19 3DW · 01767 677348
 ChequersLittleGransden; Not listed; Planning: South Cambs;
Real ale; Pizza on Fri eve (check Facebook).

quet floor with a quarter circle bar counter that appears to be of pre-war date. The bar-back fitting also looks to be of a similar date with some modern wood. There is some inter-war dado panelling and more of the heavy-duty wallpaper. The brick and wood surround fireplace also could be inter-war and has an ancient fireback, and there is some bare bench seating around the bay window.

Hanging from the ceiling is a rope which is part of the rare pub game of Ringing the Bull (see p39) – see if you can swing the metal ring and get it to land on the hook on the wall. A door at the rear leads to the small Blue Room with a bare wood floor, dado panelling painted cream, and a piano.

Closed Mon & Tue.   57 Broadway, CB3 9NQ · 01223 846004
 BlueBallFT1; Not listed; Planning: South Cambs; Real ale; Real draught cider; Meals lunch & evening Wed–Sun (not Sun eve); Accommodation (2 rooms).

Why no Mention of...?

Readers of this book familiar with the East of England might know of genuinely old pubs which aren't covered in our listings and be asking 'why not?' As a rule, the reason is that our concern is with **interiors** and many old pubs have been much altered inside – which isn't to say that they aren't still precious.

A good example is Ye Olde Bell & Steelyard in Woodbridge, Suffolk, one of very few pubs in the whole country to be listed by Historic England at Grade I. However, the reason for that grading is an extremely rare and ancient external feature – a timber-framed 'steelyard' that juts out from the building to overhang the road, and which gives the pub part of its name. A steelyard is an old form of weighing apparatus, a forerunner of the public weighbridge. The pub building itself dates from around 1550, but the interior, though perfectly pleasant, has been much opened-out and modernised.

Scole Inn, Diss

Ye Olde Bell & Steelyard, Woodbridge

Bell Inn, Stilton

Another Grade I-listed pub in the region is the Scole Inn, Diss, Norfolk. This imposing coaching inn, built in 1655, still gives you a feel of what such places were like in their heyday. It has, though, been much knocked around inside with only the enormous fireplaces in both main bars being fixtures of any age. What's more, at the time of writing, plans had been announced to convert the place (which now trades as Diss by Verve) to a 'rehabilitation centre for professionals and sports stars suffering with addictions'.

Why no Mention of...?

Pykkerell Inn, Ixworth

As mentioned on p8, many other coaching inns could be found along the Great North Road. The Bell Inn at Stilton, Cambridgeshire, is listed Grade II*, and with its huge hanging sign and honey-coloured building, certainly looks the part. The hotel section retains many fine features like sweeping staircases, inglenook fireplaces and lots of massive beams. The bar areas, though, which are our concern here, have been altered to an extent that takes them outside our criteria.

The George Hotel, Huntingdon, also served travellers on the road and is also Grade II* listed. A large, arched coach entrance leads to an atmospheric courtyard, used both as an outdoor drinking space and, occasionally, to put on Shakespeare plays. It's a fine building (as is the nearby Falcon, another old coaching inn) but the bar area is frankly anonymous.

Whilst we're in Cambridgeshire, we can't not mention the Eagle in Cambridge, arguably the city's most famous pub. It, too, started as a coaching inn, back in the 16th century, and the galleried courtyard takes you back to that era. During World War II, it was much frequented by airmen who covered the ceiling of the back room with graffiti. Then, in 1953, the peace of lunchtime drinkers was disturbed when scientists Watson and Crick burst in to announce that they had discovered the secret of life, the double helix. The original two-bar layout at the back contains a few early post-war fixtures and fittings, though nothing especially noteworthy. In 1992 the pub was greatly expanded into former office premises facing Bene't Street – the work was sensitively executed and the panelled room to the right of the entrance is most attractive.

Other superb old pub buildings, but with significantly altered interiors, are the Pykkerell Inn, Ixworth, and Swan, Lavenham, both Suffolk, and the Red Lion Hotel, Colchester (also Grade I listed).

Should you come across an East of England pub and find yourself baffled as to why we haven't included it in this book, then please get in touch (info@pubheritage. camra.org.uk). If we've checked it out and decided it doesn't meet our criteria, then we can tell you why. If it's one we simply haven't investigated, then we'll be very grateful for the lead.

Eagle, Cambridge

NEWTON

Queen's Head ★★★

A personal favourite of the editors, this has been a pub since at least 1729 and continues to be run on very traditional lines. It has been in same family ownership since 1962.

From the front door, a short passage leads to the 'Jug and Bottle' hatch, still with its two windows and bell push. To the right is the splendid, traditional, quarry-tiled public bar which is little-changed over the years. It contains a lovely, curved, high-backed settle, old dado panelling with bare bench seating, and an old wood-surround fireplace with a wood burner. Behind the lapped-wood bar counter real ales have always been sold from a stillage. In 2020 a new two-tier stillage was created to offer other beers to the Adnams ones that have been a mainstay here.

To the left of the passage is the saloon bar which was extended back to double its size in 1963. A bar counter was added for the first time and is of brick with old bottles set into it, a rare example seen in the early 1960s of which few examples remain. The inglenook fireplace at the rear was uncovered in 1963, but is not in use and you can sit in it. The front section of the saloon bar has a log fire, and another classic form of pub refitting used in the early 1960s, wood tacked to the walls to provide a mock-Tudor effect. There is bench seating in the bay window.

A gap between the piano and the back of the settle in the main bar leads to a games annexe, added in 1963, along with inside toilets. This room has dado panelling, another settle, scrubbed tables and a basic bench. You can play traditional pub games such as Devil Among the Tailors, Shove Ha'penny and darts. The Shah of Persia played darts here in 1965 – see the photograph hung above the games room window.

The Queen's Head is one of only five pubs to have featured in every edition of the *Good Beer Guide*. The food consists of sandwiches, a cheese platter, and a legendary soup – see the 'Soup of the Day' Chart.

Open Tue–Sat lunchtimes and evenings, also Sun until 4pm.
Fowlmere Road, CB22 7PG · 01223 870436
❶ Brownsouppub; Listed Grade II; Planning: South Cambs;
Real ale; Real draught cider; Meals lunch & (Thu–Sat) evening.

Saloon bar and Jug & Bottle

Public Bar

Rarely Seen Traditional Indoor Pub Games in the East of England

Pubs are places of pleasure and relaxation so it's not surprising that they've always been used for a multitude of games and entertainment. Pub games are not as popular as they were, having fallen victim to changes in pub culture and a growing focus on the provision of food, but you will certainly come across them. Some, like cards, cribbage, dominoes, or that more recent and very popular invention, the pub quiz, require little or no special provision. Others, however, do.

(Norfolk) Twister

A game played in Norfolk and only a few examples elsewhere is twister. On the ceiling of some pubs you will find a coloured wheel that usually has ten or 12 numbered segments; an arrow is spun and settles at one of them. It is a simpler version of the game of roulette and wheels

Three Horseshoes, Warham

were usually put in this location so that people couldn't cheat. Many twister boards were removed from pubs in the 1970s due to a change in gambling laws.

A featured pub with a twister is the aptly named Wheel of Fortune, Alpington (p75). There is also one at

Wheel of Fortune, Alpington

the Three Horseshoes at Warham (p119). Another pub run on very traditional lines with a twister on the ceiling is the Old Railway Tavern,

Old Railway Tavern, Eccles

Old Railway Tavern, Eccles

Eccles, which also has table skittles and shove ha'penny. There are at least another six that we are aware of in Norfolk, one at the community-owned Sorrel Horse, Shottisham, Suffolk (p72), and four more in various other parts of England.

Sorrel Horse, Shottisham

Tossing the Penny/Pitch Penny

Situated in the end of a settle, this game requires you to throw a disc (13) the size of an old penny into a 2¼-inch diameter hole cut into the settle with a drawer to catch the coins. The back of the settle is lined with lead to protect the furniture. The game can be found at the Cock, Brent Eleigh (p97), the Rose & Crown, Snettisham (p88), and the Viper, Mill Green (p58) (currently closed).

The game, which is also called Pitch Penny, can also be found at the Bull, Langley Green, and Fleur de Lys, Widdington, both Essex; Lifeboat Inn, Thornham, and Coach & Horses, Tilney St Lawrence, both Norfolk; and another in Rutland.

Cock, Brent Eleigh

Viper, Mill Green

(Suffolk) Caves

In the Crown, Bedfield, near Framlingham, Suffolk, there is the only known remaining example of the game of caves. This form of indoor quoits was invented by the landlord of The Black Boy in Bury St

Rarely Seen Traditional Indoor Pub Games in the East of England

Crown, Bedfield

Edmunds in 1930 (he even took out a patent on the game, so convinced was he of its success). It involves throwing wide rubber (quoits) rings from a distance of six feet into a wooden board with five numbered indentations or 'caves'. *Sadly, the Crown closed at the onset of Covid and there are currently no plans to reopen it.*

Ring The Bull

Ring the Bull involves swinging a 2-inch metal nose ring on the end of a rope to try to land it on an upturned hook or a horn fixed to a wall.

Blue Ball, Granchester

Appearing possibly the simplest of all pub games to play, yet it is one of the hardest to master. The first reference to the game was in the 1850s.

There are few sightings in the country. At the Blue Ball in Grantchester (p32) it is practically part of the furniture. It is also played at the Salisbury Arms in Cambridge and the Duke of Wellington, Norwich.

Northamptonshire or Hood Skittles

There are various forms of skittles played in pubs, most notably the long alley version, but there are few remaining alleys in the East of England. Just creeping into Bedfordshire is Hood Skittles, more often called Northamptonshire or Cheese Skittles as you throw what is shaped like an Edam cheese. As you enter the Cock, Broom (p23) on the left is the games room which houses a darts board and a well-polished skittles table.

Cock, Broom

The table looks like an outsized armchair with a flat, leather-covered seat for the nine pins and leather padding on the arms, back and facing edge. The attached 'hood' is made of netting on a frame and is designed to trap any flying skittles or cheeses. Pins and Cheeses are the pale-yellow plastic variety favoured in the Bedfordshire game; elsewhere they are wooden. The skittles are about 5 inches tall and tubby around the waist and made from various types of hard wood or plastic. The cheeses are thrown underhand.

Devil Among the Tailors/ Table Skittles

The other variety of skittles to be found in some East of England pubs is table skittles, also known as Devil Among the Tailors. A small wooden ball (the devil) on a light chain swivels around a pole to knock down a set of nine small pins (the tailors) arranged in a diamond formation. You have three throws to knock all skittles down. There were leagues around Bedford and Luton until recently. A pub featured in this book with table skittles ready to play is the Queen's Head, Newton (p36).

Queen's Head, Newton

Much information for this feature was found in two excellent articles in the *Eastern Daily Press* (EDP).

More details of these and other pub games can be found in *Played at the Pub: the Pub Games of Britain* (2009) by Arthur Taylor, which is available for just £10 (post free in the UK) from playedinbritain.co.uk

PETERBOROUGH

Hand & Heart ★★★

An incredibly rare survivor situated in a small terrace, the Hand & Heart is a small, purpose-rebuilt public house dating from 1938. Of two storeys in plain brick, with a flat roof, it was built for Warwick & Richardson's Brewery of Newark and is essentially intact and unaltered.

The two original front windows advertising 'Warwick's' have been replaced with similar, but not exact, copies in recent years. The front door on the left leads to a small lobby and beyond an internal door in a full-height glazed screen is the modest drinking lobby around the jug bar (off-sales), both areas with black-and-white-tiled flooring. A couple of bar stools confirms that this increasingly rare facility is in use here at times and the bell push to attract attention remains on the left. The screen in the drinking lobby can still be raised and lowered for service and the lower central panel is hinged and was used for transactions when this doubled as the off-sales, but is now permanently sealed, apparently at the insistence of 'Health & Safety'. Note the number '2', a former requirement of the licensing magistrates, on the screen in the drinking lobby.

A door on the right just short of the serving hatch leads to the public bar where the fabric and fittings from the 1930s scheme have survived very well. The bar counter has a distinctive Art Deco frontage; to the left is a door to the servery for staff which has a hatch and shelf for service.

The mirrored bar-back has succumbed to only modest changes to allow the inclusion of a fridge. The original fitted seating survives, as do the tables. The fireplace was replaced by a brick one in the 1960/70s. Note the World War II memorial on the wall of the public bar – there are only 60 or so of these in pubs in the whole of the UK.

At the rear right corner of the drinking lobby a door with 'Smoke Room' and '3' painted on it leads to a compact room which retains its full set of original fitted seating and a baffle by the door. Service is via a hatch, which until the late 1990s had a door that could be opened and closed for service. The only other lost item is the original fireplace, replaced by one in inappropriate Victorian style. You may find this room locked and used for storage but ask and the licensee will open it for you to inspect. Other doors in the drinking lobby lead to an 'inside' ladies' toilet, still with 'Ladies' painted on it, and a passageway to the 'outside' gents'.

12 Highbury Street, PE1 3BE · 01733 564653
301902744809; Not listed; Planning: Peterborough;
Real ale; Real draught cider (summer only); No food.

Public Bar

Smoke Room

HUNTINGDON

CURRENTLY CLOSED

Market Inn ★

Saloon Bar

This 1930s pub originally had four rooms, as the names in the exterior windows indicate. Inevitably for a town centre pub, windows have been lost, but high-quality replacements have been made where necessary. The saloon bar still has a 1930s vestibule entrance and a good 1930s brick fireplace; the half timbering is probably from the 1960s, likewise the fixed seating. The current main bar has 'Parlour' and 'Smoke Room' windows. The fielded panelling on two sides of the bar front has a 1930s look, though the third side is modern, indicating the bar has moved. There is a good 1930s brick fireplace, but the island bar-back is modern. The small tap room has another good 1930s brick fireplace, this one with small cupboards on each side. The plainness of the bar front suggests it's of a later date, but above it are remains of 1930s shutters. Locals have indicated that the saloon bar, parlour and smoke room were all originally served by hatches. On the first floor is a function room with an inter-war brick- and red-tiled fireplace, and a tie-beam roof.

10 Market Hill, PE29 3NJ · 01480 431183 · Not listed; Planning: Hunts; the pub is closed at the time of publication.

Public Bar

Essex

Saloon bar

AVELEY

Old Ship Inn ★★

The unassuming, rendered exterior conceals a four-room pub, the almost-intact arrangements of which date from the early 20th century: the stained-glass windows are particularly attractive. The left-hand saloon bar incorporates a former off-sales compartment (hence the disused external door) and is separated from the street-corner private bar by a full-height screen with stained glass in the upper part. The Victorian-style fireplace has a tile surround on left and right with the motif of an elegant lady on each side. On the bar counter are remains of the shutters, now converted to a pot shelf. The rear door has an etched 'Club Room' window. On the first floor is the former snooker room, which until recently housed a full-size billiards table, now replaced by two pool tables.

An old bench, still with its maker's label, is now in the garden. In the public bar the counter, with its porthole decoration, looks as though it was given something of a nautical makeover in the 1960s when such themed fitting out was

Public bar

Private bar

popular. The mirrored bar-back and brick fireplace are from the 1930s. The fourth room has a timber screen to the corridor with glazing at the top to provide borrowed light. It also has 1930s features, including an attractive inter-war-style brick fireplace.

Fireplace in former snooker room

Opens at 4pm Tue–Thu, 3pm Fri, all day Sat and Sun.
58 High Street, RM15 4AD · 07976 264053
Aveleyoldshipinn; Not listed; Planning: Thurrock;
Real ale; No food; Closed Mon.

BROADS GREEN

Walnut Tree ★★★

One of the least spoilt interiors in Essex, having been in three generations of the same family up to 2002. Overlooking the village green, this pub was built in 1888, according to the datestone high up on the right. It originally comprised the two rooms on the left – public bar and bottle and jug, now the snug – plus the outside gents' on the left, which is still in use. These two rooms are little altered. The front door leads you into the delightful snug, squeezed between the two other bars. It has a parquet floor, Victorian bar counter and a bar-back consisting of old shelves on a mirrored back. Furniture is confined to two small benches.

A part-glazed partition wall separates the snug from a simple, traditional public bar on the left with walls displaying original full-height panelling, painted deep red on the dado with cream above. Attached to the panelling are basic bench seats with padded cushions. Recently the owners have restored the glazed part of the partition near the servery to its full size. A bar counter was added in 1962. The parquet floor indicates there was none there originally, but it is not clear whether there was once a hatch. The 1950s-looking brick fireplace was actually added in the 1980s by locals and has a log fire. The modern door between the two rooms could be explained by beer only being served in the snug, which also acted as the jug and bottle prior to the counter being added in 1962.

The saloon bar on the right was originally the landlord's private parlour and just half its present size. In 1962 it was brought into pub use, adding a small counter, and, in 1981, an extension was added on the right of the building, doubling the size of the lounge and bringing the toilets inside. The handpumps are redundant as beer is fetched from the cellar.

Broads Green, CM3 1DT · 01245 360222
No Facebook; Not listed; Planning: Chelmsford; Real ale;
Real draught cider; No food; Cash only.

Lounge

Snug

Public Bar

What's in a Room Name (or Number)?

Not that long ago, all but the smallest pubs had two or more rooms. These were differentiated in terms of their ambience, clientele and, as a consequence, prices.

The most straightforward pub room was the **public bar** where the beer was a little cheaper but the fixtures and fittings fairly basic. Good examples in this book are those at the Green Dragon, Bungay (p98), and Bell, Castle Hedingham (p51). Better-appointed rooms went by a bewildering variety of names.

Old Ship Inn, Aveley

Bell, Castle Hedingham

Swan, South Wootton

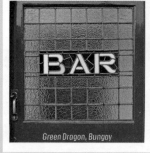
Green Dragon, Bungay

Champion of the Thames

Private bars did not require membership but were smaller than the public, and the name suggests occupancy by regulars who knew one another. The Old Ship, Aveley (p45), still has a room so named. Where such rooms were particularly small, they were known as **snugs** – see article on p108. Also on the small side are **parlours**, which again, generally, have a particular air of privacy about them; there's one at the Market Inn, Huntingdon, and

Old Ship Inn, Aveley

Buckinghamshire Arms, Blickling

Queen's Head, Tolleshunt D'Arcy

another, known as the **bar parlour**, at the Queen's Head, Tolleshunt D'Arcy (p57).

The **lounge** or **saloon/saloon bar** tended to be larger and you could expect carpets, panelling and even waiter service.

Earle Arms, Heydon

Swan, South Wootton

Old Ship Inn, Aveley

What's in a Room Name (or Number)?

The **smoking room/smoke room** is an odd one, suggesting it was where people could smoke. However, since smoking was allowed throughout the pub (until the recent smoking ban), a literal meaning makes no sense. These rooms were normally smaller than the public bar or lounge and the idea may have evolved to identify a haven where a chap (and it would have been a chap) could take his ease in the way he would have done in a gentleman's smoking room. You can find them (but certainly not smoke in them) at the Kevill Arms, Gorleston (p79), the Green Dragon, Bungay (p98), and Hand & Heart, Peterborough (p40).

Kevill Arms, Gorleston

Kevill Arms, Gorleston

Green Dragon, Bungay

Another paradoxical name is the **tap room**. You might assume this was where drinks were dispensed, but old plans of pubs, and the layouts of those with surviving tap rooms,

TAP ROOM
Green Dragon, Flaunden

indicate otherwise. It may be that the name did once describe what took place in this room, but, as with many aspects of pub lore, the title has become subverted. The suggestion we've heard that regulars would tap a coin to summon service seems fanciful given the (sometimes considerable) distance between tap rooms and serveries.

Pubs often had a **club room** or **assembly room** used for meetings or other private gatherings, generally on an upper floor. A suitably inscribed door which led to one such can be seen at the Kevill Arms, Gorleston (p79), whilst the White Hart, Grays (p53), still has a club room in use.

Old Ship Inn, Aveley

There's a particularly unusual room name – the **Ale & Spirit Bar** – at the Crown, Buntingford (p61).

You will sometimes find numbers on or above a door within a pub. There used to be (probably until the 1960s) a legal requirement on licensees to 'make entry' of their premises with HM Customs and Excise so they could check that the premises complied with the law. The process included listing all the rooms used both for the storage and the consumption of alcohol. At the Earle Arms, Heydon (p81), the lounge door sports a 2 while the saloon door at the Margaret Catchpole, Ipswich, tells you it's room 3.

Crown, Buntingford

BURNHAM-ON-CROUCH

Olde White Harte Hotel ★★

An 18th-century red-brick building which sits on the quayside alongside the River Crouch with its own jetty and water's edge seating area. It has been in the same family ownership since 1960. In 1957 it was refitted based on a ship theme and the three rooms around a central servery are barely changed since. The front bar, with river views, has a wood-block floor, a distinctive bar counter of narrow, lapped wood strips with four oblong 'box-shaped' areas at the top and a leaded screen with coloured glass panels above and to the right. Through a Tudor arch-shaped doorway is the small side bar with a similar counter, a wall with late-1950s ply panels and another wood-block floor. The rear bar, through another Tudor arch doorway, has a small bar counter more like a hatch with plain 1950s panelling, another wood-block floor, a 1950s brick fireplace, good quality fixed seating and an old tongue-and-

Side bar

Rear bar

groove panelled dado. The dining room was, until recently, the residents' lounge.

Look for the rising shutters on the bar counter which were opened for service and closed at quiet times. The ones here dating from 1957 can still be operated – very rare as most others in the country have been removed. The large, brick, inglenook fireplace was exposed in c.1970.

The Quay, CM0 8AS · 01621 782106
 Yeoldewhitehartehotel; Listed Grade II; Planning: Maldon; Real ale; Meals lunch & evening; Accommodation (15 rooms, 11 Ensuite).

Front bar

Dining room

Rare working shutters

CASTLE HEDINGHAM

Bell ★★

This former coaching inn, occupying a timber-framed 16th-century building, includes a shop on the left which is now leased out. It has an unusual layout of four rooms linked by a corridor running from the front door. Much of what you now see dates from changes in 1967, before which the main entrance was in the middle of the frontage, accessing an off-licence and rooms each side (the current public bar and saloon). Both these rooms are simply appointed with slatted-wood counters and basic bar-back shelving. The public bar has some old panelling and ale is served from casks on two wooden stillages behind the counter. The saloon bar

was expanded; the raised section was part of the kitchen pantry until the 1960s and the old meat hooks can still be seen on the beams.

The parlour on the left of the corridor only entered pub use in 1980; a glass-fronted section of wall displays the underlying wattle and daub construction. The small room at the rear called the Back Bar only came into public use in recent years. It has part-timbered walls and a hatch to the bar opposite. On the first floor, but accessed from outside, is a magnificent assembly room, built around 1790. It is called the Disraeli Theatre and Function Room, so named as it was the scene of a speech by Benjamin Disraeli. A pub theatre is planned. It was refurbished in 1980; the superb moulding on the barrel ceiling is a plaster replica of the papier-mache original.

Closed Tue, open Mon, Wed, Thu lunchtimes & evening, all day Fri, Sat, Sun closes at 8pm. · 10 St James Street, CO9 3EJ · 01787 460350 · ❀ TheBellInnCastleHedinghamHalstead; Listed Grade II; Planning: Braintree; Real ale; Meals lunch & evening Mon, Wed–Sun (not Sun eve).

Saloon bar

Public bar

COLCHESTER

Odd One Out ★★

Left-hand bars

A terraced property which became a pub in 1935 and has four separate rooms. It retains virtually all of its original 1930s fittings and layout. To the left is a bar with bare-boarded floor, solid 1930s counter, bar-back with bevelled mirror panels, brick fireplace and bench seating; note the glass snack display case on the bar. To the rear left is a small room with similar features; the high-level shelving over the counters is modern. The wall dividing these rooms was reinstated by the owner.

Rear left bar

The front right-hand small bar has a counter that has seen some changes; the front part is the 1930s original but the rest is more modern. The brick fireplace and dado panelling are the 1935 originals. There is another bar at the rear right with its original counter, a long, basic, bare bench, and a 1930s brick fireplace that has been painted red. The right-hand rooms were accessed not from the front but a side door (between the loos). In 1983 an arch-shaped doorway was cut into the wall to connect the left and right bars – the left front door is no longer in use. The gents' still retains its three big 1930s urinals.

The pub has been run on very traditional lines for over 30 years with no TV, pool, or food – just conversation and good beer. It has been leased to Colchester Brewery since 2017.

Open Mon, Tue 4–7pm; Wed, Thu 4–9pm; Fri 4–10pm, Sat 1–10pm, Sun 2–7pm.   28 Mersea Road, CO2 7ET · 07976 985083
 theoddie; Not listed; Planning: Colchester; Real ale; Real draught cider; No food.

Front right-hand bar

GOLDHANGER

Chequers ★

A 16th-/17th-century pub which in Victorian times comprised the little-changed public bar and tap room plus the wide, red-and-black quarry-tiled passageway running from the front door. Both tap room and public bar have Victorian bar counters. The public bar has a splendid fitted settle forming a partition on the passageway side; it has some windows at the top and bench seating attached. Partitions like this existed in great numbers in pubs throughout the country but are now very rare. This small room has an old brick fireplace, old dado panelling with benches attached and a part tongue-and-groove ceiling. The large rear bar came into use during the inter-war years – the counter is one of the lowest in the country! The other two rooms were residential accommodation before becoming public areas; one houses a Bar Billiards table.

Closes at 7pm Mon. 11 Church Street, CM9 8AS · 01621 788203
ChequersinnGoldhanger; Listed Grade II; Planning: Maldon; Real ale; Real draught cider; Meals lunch & evening (not Mon, Sun eve).

Front bar

Rear bar

GRAYS

White Hart ★

Once an old, weather-boarded pub, the White Hart was rebuilt by Charringtons in 1938 and retains clear evidence of the original floorplan and many original fittings. The star here is the fine, long, oak bar-back fitting in classic 1930s style which served the five rooms and off-sales. The main entrance has been blocked up, but would have led to the off-sales – now used for storage. The left-hand bar, originally two rooms, has an attractive original counter. There is a passage that links the left-hand and right-hand bars. The right-hand bar, originally two rooms, retains it's counter and fireplaces (albeit they are boarded over). The club room is still used for functions and has some old features including a dumb waiter. Access to these last three rooms was originally by the right-hand passage into the pub where 1930s tiled dado survives.

Kings Walk/Argent Street RM17 6HR · 01375 373319
The-White-Hart-Grays; Listed Grade II; Planning: Thurrock; Real ale; Meals lunch Mon–Fri.

Left-hand bar

Right-hand bar

Dispensing Differently

In most pubs, the journey of your pint of real ale from cellar to glass is straightforward. You go to the bar counter and place your order, then a handpump is pulled to fill your glass. The East of England, though, is rich in pubs where things are done a bit differently.

For a start, here we find two of the seven pubs in the country which have never had a bar counter. In times gone by, this was the arrangement in all alehouses, reflecting the domestic origins of our pubs. Counters only began to arrive in the early 19th century, bringing an element of professionalism to the sales process. Our two survivors are the Cock, Broom, Bedfordshire (p23), and the King's Head, Laxfield, Suffolk (p106).

Cock, Broom

King's Head, Laxfield

Both are great pubs in their own right, but the experience of buying a drink without anything passing over a counter or hatch is not to be missed. A third example can be found at one of the outstanding restorations we mention. When the White Horse, Sweffling, Suffolk (p121), was converted to a house, the servery was removed – and when it was restored as a pub, the lack of a

White Horse, Sweffling

counter was solved by stillaging the beer in a small alcove beyond a door in the tap room.

The Walnut Tree, Broads Green, Essex (p46), has a service method that is not greatly different. The real ales and cider are all fetched from casks in the cellar with the handpumps on the bar being 'just for show'. The Walnut Tree, Broads Green, Essex (p46), has a service method that is not greatly different. The real ales and cider are all fetched from casks in the cellar with the handpumps on the bar being 'just for show'. This also happens at the Compasses, Littley Green, Essex (p117).

Indeed, dispensing ale straight from the cask is happily not a rare sight in the region. The Queen's Head, Newton, Cambridgeshire (p36), is one of only five pubs to have been in every

Queen's Head, Newton

edition of the *Good Beer Guide* and for all those years the good beers in question have been Adnams ales served from a stillage behind the counter in the public bar. A similar arrangement applies at the Bell, Castle Hedingham, Essex (p51), where two small, wooden stillages sit behind the bar. The Butt & Oyster, Pin Mill, Suffolk (p111), seems to operate the same system, but the

Bell, Castle Hedingham

casks on the stillage are there for show, with the actual casks being in the cellar behind, the beer being dispensed via pipes through the tap.

As a rule, you will be served at the counter, but in times gone by small hatches to the servery were common and eight examples survive in pubs featured in this book. Of particular note are those at the Hand & Heart, Peterborough (p40) (for service to the rear smoke room), the Green Dragon, Wymondham,

Crown Hotel, Southwold

Hand & Heart, Peterborough

Dispensing Differently

Earle Arms, Heydon

Olde White Harte Hotel, Burnham-on-Crouch

Cross Keys, Harpenden

Norfolk (p92) (service to front room via tiny hatch cut into the servery door), the Bull, Long Melford, Suffolk (p110) (hatch from the front room with doors that can be closed) and the Golden Star, Norwich (p87) (tiny hatch with two-part sliding windows between the two rooms).

Counters often had shutters or sliding screens which were opened for service and closed at quiet times. In some cases, these still exist but no longer open, whilst elsewhere vestiges are observable. The best remaining working examples are those at the Olde White Harte Hotel, Burnham-on-Crouch (p50), where the sliding shutters on all three counters are still in use. Another excellent example is in the snug in the Maids Head Hotel, Norwich (p87), which

ale revival, though, saw brewing on the premises making a comeback and three of our featured pubs brew their own. At the Green Dragon, Bungay, Suffolk (p98), they have brewed

Green Dragon, Bungay

weekly on a seven-barrel plant since 1991. The Son of Sid's brewhouse at the Chequers, Little Gransden, Cambridgeshire (p33), dates from 2007 and their Muckcart Mild has won many awards. The Old Cross Tavern, Hertford (p118), started brewing in 2008 with 'a passion for artisanal brewing and a love of British Ales'. In all three cases, the beers are only rarely seen outside the pubs.

Bull, Long Melford

Maids Head Hotel, Norwich

has a screened hatch for service with two sliding windows.

Worthy of mention in this context are the pewter bar top and handpump base at the Cross Keys, Harpenden, Herts (p63) – very rare, if not unique.

Back in the day, many, if not most, pubs brewed their own beer, but, by the time CAMRA was formed in 1971, only four continued to do so. The real

Golden Star, Norwich

Green Dragon, Flaunden

Chequers, Little Gransden

HARLOW

White Admiral ★

Built in 1953 as the second pub in Harlow New Town, this is also one of the earliest new-build post-war pubs in the country; it remains remarkably intact. Left of the entrance, the public bar (formerly saloon) has its original counter (with later moulding on the front) and a slightly modernised bar-back. The tiled fireplace is a replacement and the fixed seating is modern. The room has been extended at the back into what was a separate small room whose original purpose is unclear (games?). The saloon (formerly public) on the right also has an original counter with new frontage plus a little-altered bar-back. The panelled dado and curved panelling above the sides of the counter are very 1950s. The off-sales survives on The Chantry side but is now used for storage.

1 Ward Hatch CM20 2NB · 01279 424839
 The-White-Admiral-The-Adders; Not listed; Planning: Harlow; No real ale; No food.

Saloon bar

Public bar

PLESHEY

Leather Bottle ★

The pub combines a single-storey building claimed to date back 400 years, and, on the left, a 19th-century yellow-brick former house. The public bar is now mainly used for dining, hence the non-traditional colour scheme and modern tables and chairs. It has a parquet floor on the left and tiling on the right. The change in ceiling height shows the room was extended at one point. Other features are painted wood panelling on the walls, traditional bench seating, and in the left portion, a low, bowed, panelled ceiling. The fireplace with a log fire originally stretched across where there is now a short passage to the lounge – the old brick on the left is the only original part remaining and there is a new brick interior. The small lounge has a brand-new counter which replaced one from c.1960 and the bar-back was replaced in the early 1980s.

The Street CM3 1HG · 01245 237291
 theleatherbottlepleshey; Listed Grade II; Planning: Chelmsford; Real ale; Meals lunch & evenings (not Mon, Tue, Sun eve).

ROCHFORD

Rose & Crown ★

An inter-war pub in the mock-Tudor style, still with a good period feel despite internal changes that took place in 2011. In the public bar the panelled counter and bar-back fittings are both inter-war though they have been reduced in length somewhat. Some of the fixed seating has also been removed, as has a brick fireplace. The off-sales, originally accessed by the middle door, has been absorbed into the public bar. The saloon has its original fielded panelled counter (with later top) and the lower part of the bar-back could also be original. Some old panelling survives, as does the parquet floor. The wall between this room and one on the far left has been removed; only a small section of wall panelling in the latter room can still be seen. Both bars retain their original gents' with dadoes of brown-glazed bricks and big urinals.

42 North Street SS4 1AD · ⊕roseandcrownrochford; Not listed; Planning: Rochford; Real ale; Real draught cider; No food.

Public bar

Saloon bar

TOLLESHUNT D'ARCY

Queen's Head ★

The Queen's Head is included in the book for its snug on the far left, a rare example of a country pub public bar hardly altered in 100 years. It has a 'Bar Parlour' etched and frosted bay window that is a replacement of the original and was fitted in the 1970s. It is a splendid little room retaining an old counter and bar-back shelves, full-height tongue-and-groove panelling with bare benches attached and two old, scrubbed tables. The flagstone floor was fitted in the 1970s on top of the original brick floor. The brick fireplace is of no great age. Elsewhere, the lounge has a good carved-wood fireplace, but the other fittings are modern. A former club room is now the small area where the dining room starts.

Opens at 3pm Mon.   15 North Street CM9 8TF · 01621 860262
⊕The-Queens-Head-Tolleshunt-Darcy; Not listed; Planning: Maldon; Real ale; Real draught cider; Meals lunch & evenings Tue–Sun (not Sun eve).

MILL GREEN

CURRENTLY CLOSED

Viper ★★★

The Viper closed in late 2019 but new owners have embarked on extensive remedial works which they have promised will preserve all the historic features whilst completing essential work 'behind the scenes'. The former description is below.

Tap room

This delightfully secluded four-roomed pub set amidst extensive woodland is little altered since 1938 when three generations of the Beard family began running it until 2005. Owned by Trumans Brewery until 1991, it narrowly escaped plans to make drastic changes in 1963.

Originally it had four doors, but the far right one was replaced by a window following subsidence after a hot, dry 1970s summer. The second door on the left leads to the tap room which is really the star attraction. It is a small space with seating round three sides near the window, a hatch to the servery, and a parquet floor and brick fireplace that appear to be refittings from around 1930. Set in the bench seating is a hole and associated drawer for the now-rare game of pitch penny. Basic pub rooms existed like this in their thousands – but now they are a great rarity.

Tap room

The left-hand front door leads to the bare-boarded public bar which became part of the pub later and retains its wall bench seating: the panelled bar counter is probably relatively recent. The third door, labelled 'Private Bar', leads to a small room which changed to its present style in the post-war period. It was decided to bring the fourth room into public use and add the panelled bar counter, still in an inter-war style, spanning the two right-hand rooms. The plaster was removed from the two right-hand rooms in the late 1970s and the fireplace in the private bar is from this time.

Public bar

Mill Green Road CM4 0PT
Listed Grade II; Planning: Brentwood.

Near right bar

Hertfordshire

Crown, Buntingford, servery

BUNTINGFORD

Crown ★

A small, mid-19th-century town centre drinkers' pub. The front doors have etched panels – 'The Crown Inn' on the left one and the rare wording of 'Ale and Spirit Bar' on the right. Two short, full-height, part-glazed baffles face you as you enter the main bar. Prior to the 1960s two short partitions formed a 'jug and bottle' with a small snug on the left and the public bar on the right. The Victorian panelled bar counter, with brackets running along its full length, remains, but the front has been shot-blasted; it was moved back about a foot in 1990. On the left, dado panelling has been painted cream and has original bench seating attached. More old dado panelling is on the right.

At the back, up a slope, is a small lounge that was a private living room until the 1980s and which had a small counter added in 2020. A function room occupies a separate weather-boarded building at the rear. It has a petanque piste in the garden. Gents' haircuts are available by appointment!

17 High Street SG9 9AB · 01763 271422
 TheCrownBuntingford; Listed Grade II; Planning: East Herts; Real ale; Meals Fri 6–9pm only.

Public bar

BUSHEY

Swan ★

Although single roomed, this is a relatively unspoilt Victorian back-street local, situated within a road of terraced housing. The 'Jug and Bottle Department' etched panel in the door indicates that an off-sales has been absorbed into the bar. A lot of the fittings – bar counter, doors, windows, wall-panelling – are, if not original, then very old. As there is no door to the rear part of the bar, it could well be that this has always been just one room. Interestingly, the gents' toilets are inside but the ladies' are 'outside', having been added at the back of the pub, possibly in the 1930s or 1950s.

25 Park Road WD23 3EE · 020 8950 2256
Web: swanpubbushey.co.uk; Not listed;
Planning: Hertsmere; Real ale; No food.

FLAUNDEN

Green Dragon ★★

Dating back to the early 17th century, this pub is included here for its barely altered 19th-century tap room on the front right-hand side. Only a handful of similar rooms or snugs formed of two or more high-backed settles can be found in the whole of the UK.

Built-in high-backed bench seating forms a passage into a small, quarry-tiled floored room. Basic bare seating is attached to very old dado panelling all around the room; two old long tables and two basic low benches complete the furnishings. Old brewery posters from Cannon, Taylor Walker and Benskins add to the atmosphere. Only two minor changes have taken place in over 100 years: as shown in the 1940s photograph of the locals listening to a wartime broadcast hanging above it, the open fireplace has had a brick infill to reduce it to a standard grate; also a small hatch has been inserted for service to the bar.

The unusual-shaped pieces of wood positioned between the mantelpiece and the ceiling look like the tilting devices for casks and would have been used in the cellar when beer was served from the cask and brought to your table in the past. (Or is it a triple gun-rest!). On the left are three linked rooms as a result of changes in 1980 – the brick bar at the front has bottles set in it. In 2020 the new owner carried out a sensitive refurbishment that exposed

Dining room

some of the timber-framed core when adding two rooms at the rear. It was rewarded with joint winner of the CAMRA Pub Designs Refurbishment Award.

Two famous customers who would have known the tap room are Joachim von Ribbentrop and the spy Guy Burgess: the former was Nazi Germany's ambassador until 1938 and had a weekend home nearby at Latimer, while the latter made his last-known British appearance here in 1951 before defecting to the Soviet Union.

Snug

Closed Mon. Flaunden Hill, HP3 0PP · 01442 832020
TheGreenDragonFlaunden; Listed Grade II; Planning: Dacorum;
Real ale; Meals lunch & evening Tue–Sun (not Sun eve).

Public bar

Snug

HARPENDEN

Cross Keys ★★

A pub since at least 1731, but notable for the virtually intact design scheme superimposed in the 1950s. A splendid survivor considering its town centre location.

Various 'olde worlde' features were introduced such as brick fireplaces with medieval overtones, leaded windows and beams. The bar on the right has a fine flagstone floor and oak beams pre-dating the makeover. The pewter top on the semi-circular bar (with pewter handpump base as well) is one of only half a dozen in the country. The counter itself has old, studded timber dividers infilled with (modern) brown tiles. Note the brass inlaid cross keys on the floor as you enter, also from the makeover. There is large, interwar-style brick fireplace and all around the room is old bare-backed fixed seating. Hanging from the beams are numerous pewter mugs, etc. on numbered hooks and there are lists of who owns them in frames on the wall.

Right-hand bar

Display case in right-hand bar

The left-hand lounge has a quarter-circle wooden counter with brick infill, a red Formica top and an unusual semi-circular brick fireplace which looks 1950s. The glass fronted display cases within both serveries may once have been used to store bottles of spirits. It still retains its outside gents' toilet.

39 High Street AL5 2SD · 01582 763989
 crosskeysharpenden; Listed Grade II; Planning: St Albans; Real ale; Meals lunch Mon–Fri.

Left-hand bar servery

Ye Oldest Pubbe?

We know little about pubs prior to Tudor times, though folk definitely enjoyed social drinking well before then. Traditions, not to say myths, have grown up over the years around certain pubs, imbuing them with an antiquity that rarely stands up to detailed scrutiny. Two of the five leading contenders are in the East of England, though neither, perhaps significantly, features elsewhere in this book.

Ye Olde Fighting Cocks in St Albans is an undeniably lovely pub with an impressive, timber-framed, octagonal former pigeon house at its core. A notice on the wall tells you 'Reputedly the Oldest Public House in Britain' and the menu proclaims it to be 'an 11th-century structure on an 8th-century site'. The site in question is near St Albans Abbey – founded in 793 – but there would have been no stone precinct structures in this position at so early a date. Excavations by a local museum suggested the foundations of the present building are from no earlier than around 1600. There may have been an earlier monastic brewhouse on the site, but that doesn't mean the building operated as a pub. Indeed, the first licensee isn't recorded until 1822. Up to 1872 the place was called the Fisherman and a full licence wasn't obtained until 1951.

The Old Ferry Boat, Holywell, Cambridgeshire, makes equally, if not more, dubious claims. These affirm variously that, according to archae-ological digs, the pub dates back to 560 or even 460, that 'local records state 1100', and that locals believe it was built around 1400 over the grave of a young woman who took her own life in 1076 after being rejected by the local woodcutter. However, the Cambridgeshire Sites and Monuments Record has no

Ye Olde Fighting Cocks, St Albans

knowledge of any archaeological investigations taking place in the vicinity. Moreover, the building presents no evidence of anything pre-dating the 17th century. Not a shred of believable evidence exists for ancient origins at what is a fine riverside pub.

The Adam & Eve in Norwich **is** featured in the book (p85). The Visit Norwich website will tell you that it 'is at least 750 years old: a Saxon well still exists below the lower bar floor, and the remains of a medieval monk were discovered during cellar excavations in the 70s'. However, the

Adam & Eve, Norwich

Ye Oldest Pubbe?

Historic England listing record states 'Former use unknown, now public house, C17 with C20 additions'. The oldest-looking part is the lower bar, but this was created from a cellar only in 1973.

Elsewhere in Norwich, the Maids Head Hotel (p87) claims to be the oldest hotel in the UK. Again, the Historic England listing description suggests otherwise – 'C15 cellars, C16 onwards with major façade alteration in the early C20'.

White Hart Hotel, St Albans

Maids Head Hotel, Norwich

Some genuinely old buildings are featured here, though the pub use started later. The Green Dragon,

Wymondham, Norfolk (p92), for instance, occupies a mid-15th-century, timber-framed building exhibiting a standard hall-house plan and with a jettied upper floor. When it became a pub is unclear – the listing description suggests it was previously a shop. It certainly hasn't been 'serving finest ales since c1371' as claimed on the pub's website. The Green Dragon is Grade II* listed, as is the White Hart Hotel, St Albans (p69), whose listing entry refers to a 'late C15 range of timber framed buildings'.

The half-timbered frontage only dates to 1935 though.

Our 'Heritage Pubs of the Future?' article (p116) also mentions a couple of pubs in ancient buildings. The Lattice House, King's Lynn, is in a timber-framed house of around 1480 to which two cross-wings were added a hundred or so years later, followed by extensions in the 19th and 20th centuries. The listing description for St Peter's Hall, St Peter South Elmham, Suffolk, states 'C15, C16 and C17 but probably with an earlier core to part'.

Green Dragon, Wymondham

St Peter's Hall, St Peter South Elmham

HATFIELD

Horse & Groom ⋆

Dating back to 1806 and with a low, timbered interior, this pub is mainly of interest for the splendid snug to the right of the entrance. Created by an old, medium-height curved settle, it has a flagstone floor, lovely inglenook fireplace (now occupied by a stove) and wall-bench seating on one side. The settle was repositioned many years ago, at the same time that the rest of the layout was opened out. Other items of interest include a copper bar top and fixed bench seating that are at least 40 years old, and a much older bench.

Open Mon 3–7pm.   21 Park Street AL9 5AT · 01707 264765
Web: horseandgroom-oldhatfield.com; Listed Grade II;
Planning: Welwyn Hatfield; Real ale; Real draught cider;
Meals (bar snacks) lunch (not Mon) & evening.

HERTFORD

Great Eastern Tavern ⋆

Built as a railway tavern in 1846 and not greatly changed since a 1940s refurbishment. The saloon on the left has a fielded panelled dado and old fixed seating around the bay windows. The counter and bar-back are from the refurbishment (the former with panels attached in the 1970s), as is the brick fireplace. On the right is the 'tap' with a sloping 1940s counter and a bar-back probably from the same period, two more brick fireplaces, fixed seating and panelled dado. This room was extended backwards in 1982–83 and all the panelling likely dates from that time.

29 Railway Place, SG13 7BS · 01992 582048
 greateasterntavernhertford; Listed Grade II;
Planning: East Herts; Real ale; No food.

HERTFORD

White Horse ★

Probably a 17th-century building, this was a pub by 1838. Until the late 1970s it was a single-bar enterprise, the original being the left-hand one with bare wood flooring and old fireplace and wall panelling; the counter and bar-back are difficult to date but may not be as old. Then the right-hand bar, with a fine fireplace, was brought into use, as was a room at the rear that houses a bar billiard table. Go upstairs on the right where the owners in 1986 brought four small, very characterful rooms with half-timbered walls into use, exposing most of the ceiling timbers and the fireplaces.

Closed Mon.   33 Castle Street, SG14 1HH · 01992 500557
⊙ thewhitehorsehertford; Listed Grade II; Planning: East Herts;
Real ale; No food.

Right-hand bar

LEY GREEN

Plough ★

Tucked away 18th-century country local situated on the border with Kings Walden village. It retains its two rooms and off-sales layout, the hatch to the latter now covered by a noticeboard. The bar on the left has an old, mirrored bar-back, a counter with Formica panels from c.1963 (the date of the handpumps), and fixed seating from a similar date. The tiny saloon at the rear has an old fireplace that has not been used for many years with seating in it; the bar counter was added in 2004. There's old dado panelling in both rooms painted a pale green colour.

Opens at 4pm Mon & Tue.   Plough Lane, SG4 8LA · 01438 871394
⊙ ploughleygreen; Listed Grade II; Planning: North Herts;
Real ale; Meals lunch & evenings.

ST ALBANS

Farriers Arms ★★

Two early-19th-century cottages were modelled as a grocers' shop and beer house around the 1860s. Remodelled by McMullens in 1926, and in 1959/60, it retains two separate bars; the off-sales was absorbed into the public bar in 1986. The three front doors indicate the public bar was formerly split into a bar, snug and off-sales. The public bar has a 1960 mirrored bar-back and only one fridge has replaced some lower bar-back shelving; also a distinctive late-1950s-style bar counter. The counter was reduced slightly on the right-hand side to create a darts area in 1986 and the removed section reused to form a canted return at this end.

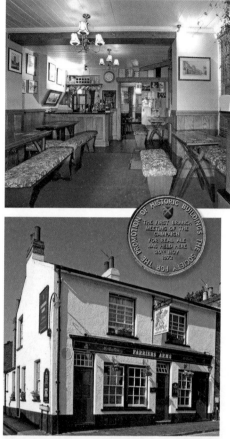

A sliding door (always open) leads to the small, upper lounge bar that retains the 1926 bar counter and an Art Deco brick fireplace now painted grey. Most dado panelling dates from 1926. Outside Gents and Ladies now under cover. A plaque commemorates the holding, on 20 November 1972, of CAMRA's first branch meeting.

Opens 5pm Mon–Fri. 32–34 Lower Dagnall Street, AL3 4PT
01727 851025 · ⓕ farriersarmsstalbans; Not listed; Planning: St Albans; Real ale; Meals lunch (not Mon, Tue). Parking difficult.

ST ALBANS

White Hart Hotel ★★

Situated on a diverted course of Roman Watling Street, this is a late-15th-century range of timber-framed buildings. A Grade II* coaching inn that had stabling for 50 horses, it has been much restored. The frontage was modernised in the 18th century but the plaster was removed in 1935 to expose the timber frame and the old windows replaced with leaded panes of 17th-century style.

The interior was refitted during the inter-war period and there have been few changes since. In the two small bars the counters and shelves attached to a part-stained and leaded partition within the servery are original features, but some modern shelves have been added. The panelling both here and in the room behind, which doubles as the hotel reception, also looks like 1930s work. Originally there were doors to the reception area at the rear of both bars but now there is a widish opening on the right-hand side. The oak-panelled walls in the two-part dining room at the back are considerably older, as is the large brick fireplace.

In 1985, whilst renovations to the White Hart Hotel were being undertaken by Benskins, the brewers, a mural of 20ft × 10ft was

discovered. It has been one of the most important examples of an Elizabethan work. Some of the mural can be seen in a corridor, some in the part of the hotel used by Pots of Art, and some now resides in St Albans Museum. Phone to check access.

23–25 Holywell Hill, AL1 1EZ · 01727 853624
whiteharthotel; Listed Grade II*; Planning: St Albans;
Real ale; Meals lunch & evening; Accommodation (15 rooms).

TROWLEY BOTTOM

Rose & Crown ★★★

A gem of a small village pub which was refitted in a simple but elegant style in the late 1950s or early 1960s and whose sheer minuteness makes it a significant survival.

The lack of recent changes is no doubt largely due to long-serving landlady Mrs Judy Wilding who, when she died in February 2016 aged 95, was probably the oldest licensee in the country. There are two rooms, a cosy public bar and an even smaller lounge, the door between them having been removed and the opening slightly enlarged.

The lounge has a quarter-circle bar counter from the 1950s with a wooden top (was it changed from a Formica one?), a 1950s brick fireplace with an electric 'log' fire in front, old fixed seating and a grandfather clock. There's a very 1960s cool-shelf in the bar-back fitting. The public bar has a panelled 1950s counter and a mirrored bar-back fitting of the same era, with

Formica on some of the shelves. Note the small till drawer hanging from the main shelf. The veneered wall panelling, wall benches attached to the front wall and brick fireplace are all part of the post-war scheme. It's the kind of pub where you are inevitably drawn into friendly conversation. The pub is open all day during the Scarecrow Festival in nearby Flamstead, which takes place on the weekend before August bank holiday.

Opens 5pm Mon–Sat.　AL3 8DP · 01582 840564
No FB/Web; Listed Grade II; Planning: Dacorum; Real ale; No food; Real ale; No food.

WARE

CURRENTLY CLOSED

Albion ★

A very old timber-framed building that has been a pub since at least 1845. Now a cosy, one-roomed local, it appears little changed since the 1950s. The 'Quality Flowers Ales' legend on the bar-back is certainly from that time (and note the glazed, leaded spirit cupboard at each end of the bar-back). The brick- and timber-built counter is certainly a period piece, as are the two fireplaces. The central ceiling beam is supposedly from the warship after which the pub is named. The entrance vestibule has some adzed timber uprights that are no doubt 1950s vintage. (*Pub closed at time of writing*)

12 Crib Street, SG12 9EX · 01920 421007
Grade II-listed; Planning: East Herts.

Community-owned Pubs

Community pub ownership is a relatively recent phenomenon. The first was actually in the East of England, the Red Lion in Preston, Hertfordshire, which was bought by villagers in 1983 from Whitbread, who were threatening to turn it into a restaurant; it is still going strong. The next 20 years saw only a few more come along, but the high-profile reopening of the Old Crown, Hesket Newmarket, Cumbria, on the cooperative model gave the sector a boost.

The next milestone was the Localism Act 2012 which introduced Assets of Community Value and the community right to bid if ACV-listed pubs were put up for sale. Even so, progress was relatively sedate and by 2017 CAMRA was aware of only 56 community-owned pubs (COPs). Since then, however, there has been a significant acceleration and we're currently aware of 156 COPs plus another 23 where the community doesn't own the pub's freehold but does control its day-to-day running. Additionally, we know of 72 active community-ownership campaigns.

32 of these COPs are in the East of England. Essex leads the way with ten and there are seven in Norfolk and six each in Suffolk and Cambridgeshire.

The most remarkable statistic around COPs is that, so far, they have a 100% success rate. A few have been sold on once the business had been re-established but all the rest have survived and thrived. It's easy to see why – the whole community will regard the pub as 'theirs', generating levels of loyalty and commitment that other operators can only dream of. Also, the pub can be guaranteed to give local people what they want, not what a pub company or freeholder is prepared to offer.

Red Lion, Preston

The only COP featured in this book is the remarkable King's Head (Low House) in Laxfield, Suffolk

King's Head, Laxfield

(p106), which has been owned by the Low House Community Interest Company since 2018. Since then, they have used the business profits to reverse the neglect to the building's fabric under previous ownership – replacing windows and doors, reroofing the accommodation building and re-decorating throughout. The latter exercise included a painstaking stripping away of the dreadful gastro-grey paint which had disfigured much of the beautiful wall panelling. They have also attended to the thatched roof which had, before 2018, turned a gruesome shade of green!

Another COP with some heritage interest is the Sorrel Horse, Shottisham, Suffolk, owned by 200 local people since 2012. They felt it necessary to make changes to the interior, including replacement of the 1950s Formica-topped bar counters. It does though retain two rooms, one with a quarry-tiled floor, old settle and the rare game of twister on the ceiling, the other (now used for dining) with dado panelling and a fine, old, brick fireplace. It also still has its toilets outside.

Sorrel Horse, Shottisham

You can discover much more about COPs at https://camra.org.uk/pubs-and-clubs/current-campaigns/save-your-local-pub/community-pub-ownership. The Plunkett Foundation is also a valuable source of information and advice – https://plunkett.co.uk/wp-content/uploads/Plunkett_How-to-set-up_Pub_final.pdf

Norfolk

Wheel of Fortune, Alpington, fireplace

ALPINGTON

Wheel of Fortune ★

Here we have perhaps the last pub in Norfolk where you can see significant remains of a Watneys 1960s refit – notably the bar-backs in the snug and left-hand bar. The former in particular is classic Watneys of the kind that once featured in hundreds of this unlamented brewery's pubs; it also has a rare surviving till drawer in the bar-back fitting. The display cases and counter in the snug are from the same era. The impressive brick and wood surround fireplace containing two display cases is from the inter-war period. The seating in the bar looks to be 1960s work; this room was later extended to the left doubling its size. On the ceiling is the Norfolk pub game of twister (see p38).

Closed Mon, opens Tue–Thu 5pm, Sun 12–7pm.
Wheel Road, NR14 7NL · 01508 492712
 wheeloffortunealpington; Not listed; Planning: South Norfolk;
Real ale; Meals Fri evening, Sat 3–8pm, Sun lunchtime.

Snug

Left-hand bar servery

BLAKENEY

Kings Arms ★

Originally three fisherman's cottages, the Kings Arms now offers several rooms, but the original layout featured just two, plus an off-sales. A wall plaque records the 1953 flood level and the bar fittings, including the lapped wood counters and red Formica-covered bar-back shelves, date from the subsequent refit. The public bar has a red quarry-tiled floor, an exposed flint wall and an old but repaired fireplace – the dado panelling and long benches are much older. Similar panelling decorates the lounge which was combined many years ago with another small room to the far right with a 1950s fireplace. Two further rooms to the left entered pub use in the 1980s and the 'Garden Room' is even more recent.

Westgate Street, NR25 7NQ · 01263 740341
 kingsarmsblakeney; Listed Grade II; Planning: North Norfolk;
Real ale; Meals breakfast, lunch and evenings;
Accommodation: 4 rooms and 3 flats.

Public bar

Lounge

BLICKLING

Buckinghamshire Arms ★

An early 18th-century brick building, now part of the Blickling Hall estate. The tiny snug, tucked between the main corridor and lounge, is the star here. It has a white-painted counter probably from the 1950s, old bar-back shelves, a 1950s brick fireplace with an ornate surround and an oddly shaped alcove. The counter in the lounge on the right is of similar vintage; the fireplace and fixed seating are old but the bar-back modern. The rooms are linked by a Norfolk pamment corridor and entrance lobby. The two-part dining room with its quarry-tiled floor and fine, old fireplaces became part of the pub until recent years. The pub was once managed by the People's Refreshment House Association, founded in 1896 to encourage temperance in inns by serving non-alcoholic beverages; look for the PRHA certificate in the corridor.

NR11 6NF · 01263 732133
 TheBucksArms; Listed Grade II; Planning: Broadland;
Real ale; Meals all day; Accommodation (4 rooms).

Lounge

Snug

BURNHAM THORPE

Lord Nelson ★

This pub was renamed in 1798 The Lord Nelson, after Vice-Admiral Horatio Nelson, who was born in the village. The Lord Nelson has seen much change in recent years, with a big extension at the back. Happily, the historic core retains much of its age-old atmosphere. An uneven, brick-floored passage leads on the left to the Nelson's Bar. Originally, there was no bar counter and drinks were brought from the cellar on a tray, but in 2002 a hole was cut in a wall to create a small counter to a new servery behind. At the same time, one of two ancient high-backed settles, attached to the ceiling with a curved iron rod, was removed.

However, as part of a restoration by Holkham Estates in 2020, a replica of the left-hand settle was installed to accompany the splendid larger one. The original tiled floor was also replaced. To the right of the passage, the Ward Room once contained many items of Nelson memorabilia. The small snug (left of the bar) was once a cellar.

Walsingham Road, PE31 8HN · 01328 854988
www.nelsonslocal.com; Listed Grade II; Planning: Kings Lynn
and West Norfolk; Real ale; Meals all day Wed to Sat & Sun lunch.

Discouraging the Demon Drink

Framed on a wall at the Buckinghamshire Arms, Blickling, Norfolk (p76), is a rather tattered certificate proudly proclaiming that 'This house is managed by the People's Refreshment House Association'. The pub nowadays will happily sell you a full range of food and drink, but that was not always so.

The PRHA, it turns out, was part of the temperance movement that began in the 1830s and flourished for over a hundred years. It was initially committed to moderation and only really opposed the drinking of spirits. However, advocates for total abstinence soon came along and crusades against the drinks trade gathered force as the century went on. The 1872 Licensing Act encouraged a reduction in pub numbers and improvements to those that remained. Alternatives to the traditional pub emerged in the shape of coffee taverns and the 'reformed' public house – the latter offering a range of delights in addition to the demon drink.

The PRHA was founded in 1896 by the Bishop of Chester and set out to acquire pubs across the country, securing over 100 by the 1920s. As most pubs were owned by brewers, properties available tended to be old inns owned by aristocratic estates – like Blickling Hall, adjacent to the Buckinghamshire Arms. The landed gentry tended to be particularly concerned about the working classes 'wasting' their money on drink. The

Buckinghamshire Arms, Blickling

Association promoted moderation and their pubs did sell alcohol – they just didn't promote it. Instead, they pushed tea, coffee, non-alcoholic drinks and food, all at reasonable prices. Managers were paid commission on sales of the latter products but not on sales of beer.

Elsewhere in the East of England, there were successful coffee taverns in many towns, Great Yarmouth, King's Lynn, Norwich and Cambridge being amongst them. Many smaller towns, and even villages, had a single tavern operated by local entrepreneurs or very small companies. Some lasted quite a long time – the Diss

Coffee Tavern didn't close until 1947 and the building survives, as do those at Hadleigh and Needham Market. At Halstead, a Temperance Hall was purpose-built but, like a number of others, incorporated a 'British Workman' temperance pub (this was effectively a brand name for a certain style of pub originating in Leeds in 1867 – there was another in Colchester).

During the First World War the Defence of the Realm Act introduced severe restrictions on licensed premises, especially opening hours. Although these were somewhat relaxed in peacetime, the increased regulation of the trade remained and this took much of the wind out of the sails of the temperance movement. (With thanks to Andrew Davison for much of this information).

Former coffee tavern, Needham Market

Halstead, Temperance Hall

CROMER

Red Lion Hotel ★

Rebuilt in 1887, this is a large hotel overlooking the sea. The public bar was, until the 1980s, a bar, snug and an off-sales on the right of the servery – note the two doors in the corner vestibule entrance, also a door in Brook Street as well as the hotel entrance on the sea-front side. The bar retains a Victorian bar counter with much surviving screenwork and a mirrored bar-back which has some modern additions. Wide openings lead to a second room which also has an old counter and a 1930s brick fireplace, this one with a non-working bell push next to it. The hotel entrance door leads into a colourful, Victorian tiled corridor. The dining room across the corridor has an excellent 1930s fireplace. The panelling around the reception area dates only from c.1985.

Brook Street, NR27 9HD · 01263 514964
 foodandrooms; Not listed; Planning: North Norfolk; Real ale; Real draught cider; Meals lunch & evening; Accommodation (14 rooms); Parking is difficult.

Public bar

Corridor

Vestibule entrance

DOWNHAM MARKET

Crown Hotel ★

A 17th-century coaching inn with a notable jettied area running to the rear. Before the 1950s the main bar was three small rooms – an extensive refit included installation of wall panelling rescued from the now-demolished Didlington Hall. The large fireplace is genuinely ancient and a smaller, curved one was added. The bar counter, made from old wooden barrels, is also from this period. A cabinet once served as a bar-back but was replaced by new shelves in the late 1980s. One further change was the removal of the dark stain from the panelling to satisfy the vogue for lighter shades. Other rooms comprise a small dining room, a function room with vaulted ceiling, a modern bar, which replaced one from the 1960s and, at the back, a Stable Restaurant.

12 Bridge Street, PE38 9DH · 01366 382322
 Crown-Hotel; Listed Grade II; Planning: Kings Lynn and West Norfolk; Real ale; Meals Sun lunch only; Accommodation (18 rooms).

GORLESTON

Kevill Arms ★

The public bar in this 1926-built Lacons house is little changed beyond absorption of the off-sales. The counter is original, albeit reduced in size and repositioned. Other features are fine fielded panelling all round, fixed seating and a notable fireplace. The original door, with stained-glass window above, is now out of use after a new internal door was created next to the fireplace. The smoke room (note the colourful stained glass window) has a 1926 tiled and wood surround fireplace, but it was extended into the former cellar in 1987. The dining room was converted from former living accommodation. Another window confirms there was a club room upstairs, now living accommodation.

Opens 7pm Mon–Fri, Sat lunch & evening, Sun all day.
67 Church Road, NR31 6LR · 01493 665937
Not listed; Planning: Great Yarmouth; No real ale; No food.

Public bar

Smoke room fireplace

GREAT YARMOUTH

Avenue ★

Built by Lacons in 1929, this mock-Tudor pub has much of period interest. The public bar has absorbed the off-sales but retains many original fittings, including half-timbering on the walls, good plasterwork decoration in the frieze area and a fine bar-back (minus the lower shelves). The counter is also original, though the leather-ette panels on the front are from the 1960s/70s, as is the top – it has also been repositioned further back. To the left, what is now a pool room also has half-timbering but has lost its fireplace. The lounge on the right was altered in the 1970s and most of the fittings are from this time. The colourful stained and leaded exterior windows throughout are a delight and two of these feature the Lacons falcon.

43 Beatty Road, NR30 4BW · 01493 843220
 avenuepubgtyar; Not listed; Planning: Great Yarmouth; Real ale; Meals lunch & evening Tue–Fri, Sat all day, Sun lunch.

A Lacons Legacy

By the 1930s, Lacons of Great Yarmouth had developed into one of East Anglia's larger breweries. In 1936 they had no fewer than 171 pubs in Yarmouth alone plus many more elsewhere in Norfolk, and in Suffolk, Cambridgeshire and even London. When taken over by Whitbread in 1965, the estate had reduced to 354 and the brewery closed in 1968. You can, though, still see their trademark falcons above the doors of pubs and ex-pubs.

Many of these pubs were designed by A.W. (Billy) Ecclestone (1901–1984). He had worked for Lacons since 1920, becoming Principal Surveyor and Architect in 1938. Ecclestone worked mostly in the neo-vernacular, Art Deco and Moderne styles, which were all popular at the time, though he put his own distinctive stamp on the buildings.

The most complete survivor that you can still visit is the remarkable, Odeon-style, beach-front extravaganza that is the Never Turn Back, Caister-on-Sea, built 1956/57 to replace a nearby hotel that became a victim of coastal erosion in 1941. You enter via a square, two-storey tower adorned with curious panels inlaid with patterns of flint, brick and stone. To one side is a tall, slim, oval sub-tower with the Lacons falcon perched on top. Right and left are the single-storey, flat-roofed bars, each with a veranda supported by brick pillars. The internal layout is largely unchanged though most of

Never Turn Back, Caister-on-Sea

the fixtures and fittings are recent. The counter in the public bar has its original brick and pebble inlays, but, sadly, these were covered over with wood panels in 2011. The north sections of both rooms extended backwards, partitioned by sliding doors in the public bar and roller shutters in the lounge; the doors in the former have been removed and the area is now a performance space whilst the lounge area is fully separated and used for storage.

Nearby is the Ship Inn, where Billy supervised an extension and renovation in 1956–8. The extension, to the front left of the pub, houses a fully panelled room with brick and pebble fireplace; other than most panelling being painted and the ladies' toilet in one corner being removed, it is little changed. The large photos both here and in the main bar are of ships built for the

Ship, Caister-on-Sea

Heylett family who ran the pub from 1912 to 1977. Many of the fittings in the bar, including the counter, are from the 1950s renovations.

Billy was an enthusiast for large tiled panels made by Carters of Poole. A good example can be found at the Clipper Schooner in Yarmouth, depicting the eponymous sailing vessel

and helpfully dated 1938. At the Iron Duke, Norwich (now the Duke of Wellington), you can see a 40-tile bust of the hero himself above the door.

Finally, to another Iron Duke, this one back in Yarmouth. Work started here in the late 1930s, but, because of the war, opening was delayed to 1948. It is late Art Deco in appearance with streamlined styling, superb brickwork and abundant Moderne features. However, in the mid-2000s, it was bought and closed by the owners of the holiday camp next door, who wanted to redevelop the site. Thanks to the great work of the Friends of the Iron Duke, the building was first listed then bought by the council and put in the hands of the local Preservation Trust. At the time of writing, uncertainty surrounds its future though the Friends are pressing hard for a return to pub use. Many original features apparently survive inside.

GREAT YARMOUTH

Coach & Horses ★

Although built around 1850, the glazed brick frontage here is early 20th century and the top storey is a post-war replacement following bomb damage. Star attraction is the small room rear-left with its fielded panelled walls to picture-frame height, a hatch for service and a bar-back (probably from 1958) decorated with small pieces of glass. The L-shape of the bar betrays the removal of the off-sales shop whose door is still visible outside. The bar counter is old (with front panels added some 30 years ago) and the bar-back, dado panelling and fixed seating all date back at least 50 years. A hole was cut in the wall between the lounge and former off-sales when the latter was combined with the public bar. Pity that much of the woodwork has been painted over.

196/197 Northgate Street, NR30 1DB · 01493 844374
Not listed; Planning: Great Yarmouth; Real ale; No food.

Lounge

Rear left room

HEYDON

Earle Arms ★

An 18th-century pub in an estate village. A large entrance lobby with old, panelled dado leads, on the right, to the former public bar, mainly used as a dining room. It has the same dado panelling, an old brick fireplace with curious cupboards on each side and a counter which is more like a hatch with no dispensers – the handpumps are next to the old bar-back shelving which is rarely seen. Left of the lobby is the current bar, once the lounge, with '2' on the door (unusually, on both sides), a pamment floor and an old brick fireplace; the brick bar dates only from 2006. A further room at the rear right brought into pub use has a 1950s fireplace.

Closed Mon, Tue & Sun evening.
The Street, NR11 6AD · 01263 587391
🅕 theearlearms; Listed Grade II; Planning: Broadland; Real ale; Meals Wed to Sat lunch & evening, Sun lunch.

Hatch in former public bar

Fireplace in current bar

Fireplace in former public bar

KENNINGHALL

Red Lion ★★

The snug to the right of the entrance is one of Norfolk's finest old pub rooms and creates a wonderful, intimate drinking space. It has curved partition walling formed by high-backed settle seating. There are only a dozen similar rooms left in the whole of the UK. Until recently the timbers were painted white, which has been subject to sand blasting. The metal grille on the corner is a modern insertion, presumably to aid supervision. More curious is the little, rectangular, hinged opening over the doorway for which no logical explanation has been put forward. The floor of the corridor and snug are laid with traditional, large, Norfolk terracotta tiles known as pamments. There is an old, large, brick and wood surround fireplace with a mantleshelf that almost reaches the ceiling. It houses a wood burner. The pub, and in particular the snug, is a remarkable survivor, having been shut for seven years until 1997.

The public bar at the rear left has fittings from 1997. Along the passage to the right there is a dining room at the rear that was formally living quarters, and has stable-like seating areas and a large fireplace.

Opens 4pm Tue–Thu. East Church Street, NR16 2EP · 01953 887849 · ⊕redlionkenninghall; Listed Grade II; Planning: Breckland; Real ale; Meals lunch and evening Mon & Thu–Sat, also Sun lunch.

Snug

Public bar

Snug

LARLING

Angel ★

Early 17th-century pub – now bypassed – which has been in the Stammers family since 1913 with a gap between 1949 and 1983. It still retains the off-sales hatch in the short passage as you enter, with the public bar on the left and lounge on the right. In the lounge the oak-panelled walls, bar-back, slatted bar counter and fixed seating are from an inter-war refurbishment. In the bar the 1930s bar-back has some modern additions; the bar counter was replaced in 1983 and the 1930s brick fireplace was increased in size. The two small rear rooms have been brought into use more recently and have no old fittings. The Angel sells 100 malt whiskies and holds its own beer festival in August.

Off A11, NR16 2QU · 01953 717963
AngelLarling; Listed Grade II; Planning: Breckland; Real ale; Real draught cider; Meals lunch & evening; Accommodation (5 rooms, no breakfast).

Lounge

Public bar

Traditional Indoor Pub Games in the East of England

Darts

Darts is now by far the best-known pub game. Back in its glory days of the late 1970s and early 1980s 10% of the population, according to a Sports Council survey, played darts (not all in pubs of course), making it more popular than football and second only to fishing as a participation sport. A 2006 survey found dartboards in 53% of pubs. You will still find dartboards in huge numbers of pubs. The standard board today has a 20 at the top, double and treble rings, and an inner (50) and outer (25) bull's eye.

There are some regional boards in use: one is the Ipswich (or Suffolk) Fives board where the sections are wider and the numbers are multiples of five. There is only one league remaining which uses a Fives board, the Ipswich Mencap Ladies' League. There are Fives boards and league teams at the Margaret Catchpole (p104) and Golden Hind in Ipswich (p101). There are Fives boards in East London which have narrower double and treble scoring segments than that of the Ipswich Fives.

Margaret Catchpole, Ipswich

Shove Ha'penny

A Shove Ha'penny board is usually wood, but can be slate, etc. There are nine beds, each measuring 1¼ in deep, just enough to accommodate one halfpenny (or a modern 2p piece). It has a semi-circular ridge surrounding the beds to stop the

Queen's Head, Newton

coins from sliding off. You place a halfpenny with one side smooth at the foot of a long, smooth board and each player in turn strikes it with the palm (heel) of your hand so it slides towards the top. If a coin ends up touching the line, even by a whisker, it does not count.

It has suffered a massive decline in popularity, with barely any leagues remaining. Pubs featured in this guide with boards available to play are the Queen's Head, Newton (p36), the Old Railway Tavern, Eccles (see above); and the Cock, Brent Eleigh (p97), where it is carved into a table.

Another game carved into a table featured in this book is believed to be called 'Go' and can be found at the King's Head, Laxfield (p106).

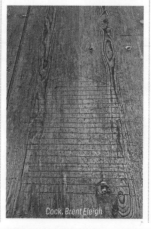
Cock, Brent Eleigh

Bar Billiards

Bar billiards, thought to have been introduced from Belgium in the 1930s, can be found in pubs in the East of England. The game was at its peak in the early 1960s, and in recent years tables have been removed for more dining tables. Pubs featured in this guide with bar billiards tables include the Golden Star, Norwich (p87), Chequers, Goldhanger (p53) and the White Horse, Hertford (p67).

Golden Star, Norwich

Billiards/Snooker

In late-Victorian times and the early twentieth century full-sized billiards was widely played in British pubs in rooms large enough to house tables for the purpose. There was a snooker table in the upstairs room at Old Ship, Aveley, but is has recently been replaced by two pool tables.

Cards

The most played card game in pubs is crib, short for cribbage. The card game **Phat**, which is very popular in Herefordshire, is played at the Buck, Rumburgh (p112) on a Sunday evening.

Buck, Rumburgh

The card game **Euchre**, very popular in Devon and Cornwall, has an outpost in Great Yarmouth. In 2016 there were six pubs still in Yarmouth's Euchre League, including the Kevill Arms, Gorleston (p79).

NORWICH

Adam & Eve ★

A 17th- century brick-and-flint building which has been a pub for some considerable time. The front door leads into the top bar with two low, old settles attached to the ceiling. This small, quarry-tiled room has some old dado panelling, but the bar counter and bar-back are new. It seems to have been subdivided as the floor markings suggest the position of more partitions in the past. The most intact part of the pub is the small snug situated in a 1930s extension. It retains its parquet floor, period brick fireplace and fixed seating, but the dado panelling is new. The lower bar was created in 1973 from the former cellar and also has modern fittings.

Open Mon–Thu 12–9pm, Sun 12–7pm.
17 Bishopgate, NR3 1RZ · 01603 667423
 theadamandevenorwich; Listed Grade II; Planning: Norwich; Real ale; Meals Mon–Sat 12–6pm; Sun 12–4pm.

Berstrete Gates ★

Refitted in the 1930s (when the flat roof extension was added), this pub retains three rooms and plenty of inter-war fittings. The main bar sports fielded panelling, brick fireplace, leaded windows and a 1930s panelled counter; the bar-back is no doubt from the same era but has some modern items such as the small glass pieces from the 1960s (or later). This room has, though, been enlarged in recent years by incorporation of a lobby area. On the right, a splendid small snug has more oak panels on the walls, painted over in recent years, and a 1930s brick fireplace. The small dining room on the rear left has a 1930s wood surround fireplace with new tiles and is served by a hatch/doorway. The inn sign, a bas-relief panel by local artist John Moray-Smith (see feature p90) was restored in 2019, funded by Bracondale Residents Association and others.

174 Ber Street, NR1 3EN · 01603 620623
 Berstrete-gates-public-house; Not listed; Planning: Norwich; No Real ale; No food.

Top bar

Snug

Public bar servery

Snug

Hatch in Dining room

NORWICH

Gatehouse ★★

An attractive, 'improved' public house in a free vernacular style, completed in 1934 for Norwich brewers Morgans, and retains most of its original fixtures and fittings. In the 1970s the smoke room on the left and the off-sales were amalgamated. The public bar has its original counter here and back fitting with an old till drawer and a cigar cabinet with leaded windows. It has a high ceiling imitating an open roof space, the original brick fireplace and 1930s fixed seating.

The former smoke room part is in a splendid semi-circular tower-like section (which has its own entrance). The Tudor Arch stone and brick fireplace is a notable feature of this room. It has three-quarter-height panelling, a Tudor-style fireplace in a panelled surround set within a curved wall, and the old bell push. On the right the saloon bar has more panelling and is served by a hatch to the side of the servery.

Throughout the pub there is an attractive, narrow, decorative plaster frieze with depictions of hops, flowers and leaves. The mullioned

Public bar

windows feature stained-glass roundels depicting symbols connected with the Bayeaux Tapestry. At the back are a loggia and extensive gardens leading down to the River Wensum.

The pub was Grade II listed as a result of Historic England's Interwar Pub Project and nominated by CAMRA.

391 Dereham Road, NR5 8QJ · 01603 620340
Listed Grade II; Planning: Norwich; Real ale; No food.

Public bar

Smoke room

NORWICH

Golden Star ★

A 17th-century building that became a pub in the 19th century. The main bar was once two rooms and an off-sales, as indicated by the markings on the wall, ceiling and counter. It retains what may be the original counter with ornate brackets all along the top, but the bar-back has an old, lower part with a top part added around 1984. Some of the wall panelling is old and the fixed seating on the right is at least 40 years old. The rear bar housed the Golden Star brewery in the late 70s/early 80 and was converted to a bar in 1984; it houses a bar billiards table. The bar counter is old but imported and the bar-back was added in 1984. There is an old baffle/short partition and a tiny hatch with two-part sliding window between the two rooms.

57 Colegate, NR3 1DD · 01603 632447
 goldenstarnorwich; Listed Grade II; Planning: Norwich; Real ale; Meals lunch & evening (not Sun evening).

Main bar

Hatch

Maids Head Hotel ★

A large hotel in a building dating from the 16th century but with major façade changes in the 20th century. Head for the main bar at the rear of the hotel with an entrance in Wensum Street. It has an old brick fireplace with wood surround and plentiful panelling and internal dimpled-glass windows; the counter, however, is modern, as is the mirrored bar-back. The star here is the delightful wood-panelled snug whose screened service hatch has two sliding windows; it is intact though nearly always left open. Other attractive features include an old fireplace with Delft tiles, three bell pushes, a tiny letter box and fitted cabinets in the wall. The Oak Room suite has fielded panelled walls which look inter-war, and some bell pushes. Situated in the corridor the Norwich Panorama bas-relief panel by John Moray-Smith (see feature p90) was previously at the Cock Tavern in King Street.

20 Tombland, NR3 1LB · 01603 209955
 maidsheadhotel; Listed Grade II; Planning: Norwich; Real ale; Meals lunch & evening; Accommodation (84 rooms).

Fireplace in Snug

NORWICH

Whalebone ★

Built in 1878–80, the Whalebone is included for its public bar and in particular the splendid, original and rare bar-back advertising 'Bullard & Son', 'Ales', '& Stout' in narrow, mirrored panels along the top and also with four narrow, vertical, mirror panels. The bar counter is original with ornate brackets along the top, but with a new top, as is the red-and-black-diamond quarry-tiled floor in the entrance area. The off-sales was situated opposite the side door. Another small room to the right of the bar is also original. The pub has been much extended and refurbished, but this does not impact on the old parts.

Opens at 2pm Mon–Thu and at 1pm on Fri.
144 Magdalen Road, NR3 4BA · 01603 425482
WhaleboneFreehouse; Not listed; Planning: Norwich; Real ale;
Meals street food outside Tue, Wed, Thu, Sat evenings.

SNETTISHAM

Rose & Crown ★

The best part of this early-17th-century village inn is the small, beamed front bar with an unusual split door, its uneven pamment and its brick floor. It has an ancient, high-backed settle, very old fixed seating and a large, brick, inglenook fireplace with side oven. The bar counter, from old wooden vessels, has also been there some time. To the left, a small bar has an old fireplace, bell push, and somewhat newer counter and seating. The small dining room far left has come into pub use more recently. A tiled passage leads to the bare-boarded rear bar with splendid, old brick fireplace whose panelled counter looks inter-war. About 30 years ago the pub was greatly extended to create dining spaces, but none of this work impinged adversely on the historic core.

Old Church Road, PE31 7LX · 01485 541382
rosecrownsnetti; Listed Grade II; Planning: Kings Lynn and
West Norfolk; Real ale; Meals lunch & evening, also breakfast;
Accommodation (16 rooms).

Front bar

Left-hand bar

Ancient settle

SOUTH WOOTTON

Swan Inn ★

This brick and Norfolk carrstone building was purchased by Steward & Patteson in 1929 who shortly afterwards refitted and extended it. The public bar on the left has a bare wood floor, a canted bar counter that looks very 1930s but may be a replacement, a bar-back mixing 1930s and more recent work, and inter-war bench seating and brick fireplace. A dado of 1930s panelling is painted cream where a section of the bench seating has been removed. The smoke room on the right is completely covered in 1930s wall panelling which indicates the room has been this size since that time. The bar-back is the original with a mirrored back, as is the counter. Also of note are the fielded panelled doors with a glazed panel in the top and numbers '1' and '2', a good high-backed bench as you enter, and seating probably from the 1930s. A 1960s-looking fireplace on the far right has a built-in clock above it. An off-sales hatch between the two rooms has been lost.

21 Nursery Lane, PE30 3NG · 01553 672084
www.swaninnsouthwootton.co.uk; Not listed; Planning: Kings Lynn and West Norfolk; Real ale; Meals lunch & evening.

Smoke room

Public bar

THORPE ST ANDREW

Gordon ★

A mock-Tudor pub built by Bullards in 1934 and allegedly incorporating some reclaimed doors and windows reputedly from the old city hall. The exterior doors have numbers on the inside of them, a requirement of the licensing magistrates. The three original rooms still exist, but gaps were cut into the dividing walls in the 1970s, and, on the far left, a former private room has come into pub use. The main bar has a brick counter, impressive brick fireplace with a mantelpiece that almost reaches the ceiling, and some fielded panelling within the servery. The bar-back, though, is mostly modern. A widish gap leads to the right-hand room with another curved, original brick counter and a brick dado. The left-hand bar looks like it has been extended into the former off-sales and a curved, brick counter added in the style of the original ones elsewhere. This bar has another impressive brick fireplace and a brick dado. Sadly, the once colourful floral-design plaster frieze that runs through the original three rooms has recently been painted over in blue.

Closed Mon, opens at 2pm Tue–Fri. 88 Gordon Avenue, NR7 0DR 01604 300901 · ✆thegordonnorwich; Not listed; Planning: Norwich; Real ale; No food.

Main bar

The Unique Bas-relief Panels by John Moray-Smith

Between 1937 and 1958, local artist John Moray-Smith produced unique, vivid, highly detailed and often huge three-dimensional panels (*bas-reliefs*) for Morgans Brewery of Norwich. Installed both outside and inside their pubs in Norwich and elsewhere in Norfolk, they distinguished the brewery's pubs with locally relevant, strong, visual images depicting everyday scenes. Many survive, some on public view in and on pubs; others now in museums; and, sadly, the whereabouts of others are unknown.

An example of an exterior sign of 1937 is that on the Berstrete Gates, Norwich (p85) depicting the gates themselves – the colours have faded.

Berstrete Gates, Norwich

There are two other exterior works to be found on Norwich pubs: one, reputed to weigh a ton, is on the Coachmakers Arms, St Stephens Road, and pictures St Stephen's Gates in the late 1600s. Having suffered from traffic fumes, it was restored in 2013 by the Norwich Society. Another of 1939 is on the prince of Denmark, Sprowston Road, and shows the Prince on a white

Maids Head Hotel, Norwich

charger. Measuring 4 metres by 3 metres, it was repainted in 2015.

An interior panel example is that entitled 'The Norwich Panorama', commissioned for the Cock Inn in

King Street, Norwich. in the mid-1940s. After the pub closed, it spent time at Caistor Hall Hotel until bought and restored by the Norwich Society. Measuring 2.5 metres by 1.5 metres, it is of moulded plaster and very heavy. This remarkable and highly colourful work of art is now displayed in the main passage of the Maids Head Hotel, Norwich (p87).

The biggest display of panels in a pub is the five (of originally six) on

Woolpack, Norwich

Coachmakers Arms, Norwich

Woolpack, Norwich

The Unique Bas-relief Panels by John Moray-Smith

the walls of the Woolpack, Golden Ball Street, Norwich. They depict sheep farming; a sheep market; wool dyeing and packing; sheep shearing; and export of wool. Nowadays, plastic screens protect them after one was damaged by a flying beer glass!

Three (of originally four) panels produced for the Ship Hotel, Cromer, in 1951 are on display in Cromer Museum, Tucker Street, Cromer, NR27 9HB (01263 513543), which has a small admission fee. Six panels produced in 1948 for the Jolly Farmers, Lynn, are being stored at Gressenhall Farm & Workhouse Museum of Norfolk Life, near Dereham NR20 4DR (01362 869263). Contact the museum for viewing details of these, and also two of originally six panels produced in 1950 for the Men of March, March (another of the Men of March panels is on display in March Museum).

Panels on display in Cromer Museum

There is an excellent, fully illustrated booklet entitled *John Moray-Smith: the eccentric Norwich artist who brought individuality to our pubs with extraordinary panels showing local scenes through the ages* by Paul Burall (Norwich Society, 2017) ISBN 978-0-9956322-0-2, which can be purchased from City Bookshop Norwich www.citybookshopnorwich.co.uk, for £3.00 plus postage.

WYMONDHAM

Green Dragon ★★

The Green Dragon occupies a mid-15th-century timber-framed building with flint and brick built to a standard hall-house plan. Up until 1993 it had one of the most impressive historic interiors in the whole of Norfolk and even today it is of significant interest. The front door leads into a passage, at the rear of which is the bar which is almost split into two by wooden partitions forming settle seating to the left and right. The latticed glass panels at the top of both partitions were added in the 1930s. The central section, which reached the ceiling, was sadly removed by a previous licensee in 1993. Hundreds of such snugs surrounding a fireplace once existed, but the vast majority have been opened up to create one large room. What remains here is a remarkable survivor (see feature p108). It has a red-quarry-tiled floor and a wide, brick, inglenook fireplace which is a 1930s replacement. The mantelpiece, supported on three carved grotesque corbels, is also inter-war work though with a medieval flavour.

The screened servery looks like inter-war work, with a panelled bar counter and old shelving. The front part of the building was originally a shop and is now more of a dining room with exposed timber framing. Recently a 1930s fireplace has been replaced by a reclaimed

Front room

Settle in bar room

Servery

brick one. A passage at the rear leads to a small dining room brought into use in recent years. Upstairs is a large bare wood floored room called The Den with an old wood surround fireplace but modern servery.

6 Church Street, NR18 0PH · 01953 607907
greendragonnorfolk.co.uk; Listed Grade II*; Planning: South Norfolk; Real ale; Meals lunch & evening Mon–Thu, Fri & Sat all day, Sun lunch.

Bar room

SHERINGHAM

CURRENTLY CLOSED

Dunstable Arms ★

Public bar

This pub has been closed for some time but is being advertised by its owners for lease or sale. The previous description is below.

Rebuilt in 1931 in Tudor-style, this attractive pub has three rooms and retains many original features. On the left is an extension added in 1945/6 in a similar style (the pub was reportedly damaged by bombing in 1940). The only recent change is the cutting of a doorway between the two bars – until then you could only access each bar via its own external door. On the right, the saloon bar has its original counter, fireplace and parquet floor. When built, a wooden partition separated it from the rear 'club room'. You can still see signs of where the partition ran, and when it was removed in the mid-1980s the timber was reused for the present bar-back fitting in the public bar. The combined room is now a dining area; it is in 'Tudor hall' style with a high ceiling and exposed timber beams. It has a magnificent full-height chimney breast in brick and tile. In the public bar, original features include the

unusual brick bar counter recently painted white, brick fireplace, timber frieze, parquet floor and some fixed seating. The pool room beyond the brick arch is an amalgamation of the old off-sales and a previously private room.

27 Cromer Road, NR26 8AB   Not listed; Planning: North Norfolk.

Saloon bar

Traditional Outdoor Pub Games in the East of England

Steel Quoits (Suffolk & North Essex)
Steel Quoits is a traditional game, which involves throwing Steel Rings weighing about 3lb each into a clay bed over a distance of 18 yards. It is a game that at one time was played throughout Suffolk and in north Essex.

The 14th British Quoits Championships were held in 2019 on Holbrook village green in Suffolk with participants from clubs in Essex, Suffolk, Wales and Scotland. The Swan pub was the base for the club for many years.

Margaret Catchpole, Ipswich

There was a pitch at the Golden Hind, Ipswich until 2018 when the land alongside the pub was sold for housing. There is a shorter form of the game in the North of England (over 11 yards) with a different weight of quoit.

Bowls

Arguably Britain's longest established sport, dating back to the 13th century. Since 1960s hundreds of greens have been turned into either car parks or beer gardens, or more often sold off for development. Special mention needs to be made of the green at the Margaret Catchpole, Ipswich (p104) built by the Cobbold Brewery, the owners of the pub, in 1948. It was handed over to The Margaret Catchpole Bowls Club in 1950, which is still active.

We are only aware of three other bowling greens in the East of England: at the Kings Head Hotel, North Elmham; Angel Inn, Swanton Morley; and the White Hart, Warboys.

Petanque/Boules

Originating in France, the first *terrains de petanque* to be laid in a pub was in Braintree, Essex, in the 1960s. A third to a half of clubs affiliated to the British Petanque Federation use terrains laid at pubs, though some licensees have decided that the players do not drink enough to justify the space and upkeep of a terrain.

Three boules per player can be rolled or thrown, even in a high trajectory, and the boules themselves have no bias, unlike bowls. They are smaller – 70.5–80mm in diameter – metallic, and must be stamped with the weight (650–800g). Before releasing the boule a player must stand with both feet inside a circle

Crown, Buntingford

measuring 235–250cm in diameter. The aim is to land one of the boules as close as possible to the jack, which has been thrown 6–10m from the circle.

There is a piste at the Crown, Buntingford (p61).

Dwile Flonking

The game of Dwile Flonking was invented by some apprentices at Clays Printers in Bungay, Suffolk. It involves two teams of 12 players with each taking a turn to dance around the other while attempting to avoid a beer-soaked dwyle (cloth) thrown by a member of the non-dancing team.

The Waveney Valley Dwile Flonking Association holds an annual Bungay v Beccles match. There are at least two games a year at the Lewes Arms, Lewes, East Sussex, where it is called dwyle flunking. Our photo is of a game at the Red Lion, Snargate, in 2011, to celebrate the pub being in the same family for 100 years.

Suffolk

Cock, Brent Eleigh, 'old bar'

BRENT ELEIGH

Cock ★★★

The book *The Quest for the Perfect Pub* by Nick and Charlie Hurt, about their search for the last remaining unspoilt pubs in the country, identified this as being the perfect pub they had been looking for.

An attractive, thatched, wayside 18th-century pub, the Cock retains its two-room and off-sales layout. The pink rendering conceals a timber-frame which could be older. Its little-altered interior results from it being run by some long-serving licensees such as the Beere family who ran it for 50 years. The most famous of its former licensees is Sam Potter who ran it for 20 years until 1989 and the pub is still called 'Potter's Bar' by some locals!

The small 'old bar' on the right has its own front door and is also accessed via a narrow door from the main left-hand bar. It has a small bar counter with genuinely old woodwork, and a set of old bar-back shelves with a till drawer in it. This small, quarry-tiled room has a low, tongue-and-groove panelled ceiling, old wooden panelling in the dado around the room with bare wall benches attached on the left wall side, an old bench on the right near the servery and a small shelf to rest your drinks, a large, scrubbed table, and an old fireplace with a fine wood surround with what looks like 1930s brick interior.

The main bar on the left is accessed from the corner door and has a quarry-tiled floor and a 1930s brick fireplace with a coal fire; seating consists of two basic bare benches, an assortment of chairs and a few bar stools. The only changes to the interior took place in 1976 – previously service here was via a hatch. Half of the present servery was originally taken up by the off-sales, but the reduced off-sales area remains, with its twin doors for service, to the left and is entered by a side door further from the road. The counter and bar-back shelves in the main public bar date from 1976. In the end of one of the benches is a hole for the rare pub game of tossing the penny (see p38). Carved on the scrubbed table is an early form of shove ha'penny (see p84); the pub also has bagatelle. It retains its outside ladies' and gents'.

Open Mon–Thu 12–3pm, 5–11pm.   Lavenham Road (A1141), CO10 9PB · 01787 247371 · No FB/Web; Listed Grade II; Planning: Babergh; Real ale; Real draught cider; Meals Sun lunch 12–4pm, sandwiches at other times.

Main bar

BUNGAY

Green Dragon ★

Late Victorian pub refitted in the 1930s, with the layout from that time still clearly visible. The front doors have good 'Bar' and 'Smoke Room' leaded windows. The quarry-tiled bar retains its inter-war counter, mirrored bar-back and fixed seating in the bay window. The smoke room also has its 1930s counter, though, as in the bar, it has been refronted, albeit in sympathetic style. The mirrored bar-back and wood-surround fireplace are of similar vintage. A third room on the right has come into use more recently. The door on the left-hand side of the pub led to an off-sales through a door, but this is no longer open. The pub has been brewing its own beers on a seven-barrel plant since 1991.

29 Broad Street, NR35 1EF · 01986 892681
 greendragonbungay; Not listed; Planning: East Suffolk;
Real ale; Real draught cider; Meals Thu–Sat 12–8pm.

Bar

Seating in bar

BURY ST EDMUNDS

Nutshell ★★★

The 'tiniest pub in the country'* at a mere 15ft × 8ft internally. The three-storied, timber-framed and rendered building itself is probably early- to mid-19th century. It is very shop-like with large windows enabling you to see the whole of the interior without stepping over the threshold.

Inside are an old counter and bar-back shelves plus seating on bare benches attached to an old, panelled dado painted brown. The answer to the question 'how many people can you get into the Nutshell?' is up to 20 (the record is 102, plus a dog called Blob, set on 10 March 1984, beating the previous record by one).

The property, previously a newsagent's, was taken over in 1873 by a John Stebbing who opened it as a beerhouse. As with many other pubs, it boasted a collection of curiosities including cork models made by Mr Stebbing and a stuffed, three-legged chicken. On display is a 400-year-old mummified cat found behind the fireplace in 1935 (they were a way of warding off evil spirits from houses). Various 'smallest pub' souvenirs are on sale such as t-shirts, polo shirts, pottery mugs and fridge magnets. There is just one

toilet – a WC up the narrow staircase on the first floor. Ask to see the visitors' book. A number of 'smallest pub' souvenirs are on sale.

In 2021 the pub was granted permission to have an outside area, which operates with table service. As there is only one member of staff, when the outside area is operating you stand just inside the pub to order your drink, then sit outside and your drink is brought to you. You will find the areas to the left and right of the entrance will be roped off. This will the case if the weather is fine, or not too cold. Only if the outside area is not operating are you able to spend any time inside the pub. May close early if quiet.

Other claimants are the Signal Box Inn, Cleethorpes, which opened in 2006, with a floor area of just 8ft × 8ft, but it is only open from Easter to Mid-October. In 2016 the Little Prince, Margate, measuring 11ft × 6ft, with space for about six people, was recognised as the UK's smallest by Guinness Book of World Records. The micropub, Platform 3, Claygate, Surrey, is so tiny there is only space for one customer to order a drink and everyone drinks outside!

17 The Traverse, IP33 1BJ · 01284 764867 · ⓕthenutshellpub;
Listed Grade II; Planning: West Suffolk; Real ale; No food.

BURY ST EDMUNDS

Rose & Crown ★★

This 17th-century building with a 19th-century exterior of red brick including ornamental tiles on the upper storey has been a pub since at least 1913. It was run by the same family for 44 years until 2019. The highlight is the surviving off-sales situated between the two bars. This is a tiny, narrow room, more like a passage, with a dado of tongue-and-groove panelling. At the end is an old counter with four handpumps and a part-mirrored bar-back. Amazingly, the off-sales is still in use, mainly for confectionery sales, but the occasional jug is still filled with cask ale.

Public bar

The oddly shaped public bar is a result of combining it with a private room in 197/6. The right-hand part of the bar counter was actually added in 1976, but it looks almost identical to the left-hand section. The bar-back shelving and part-panelled walls with benches attached date from inter-war times.

The lounge on the left has more old tongue-and-groove panelling, an old bar counter with a modern front added, and an old mirrored bar-back fitting; the pot shelf is a modern addition.

Opens 3.30pm Mon, Tue & Thu, closes Sun 6pm. 48 Whiting Street, IP33 1NP · 01284 361336 · ⓕ roseandcrownbse; Listed Grade II; Planning: West Suffolk; Real ale; No food.

IPSWICH

Golden Hind ★

In the 1930s the Tollemache brewery of Ipswich underwent a large expansion and built several vast mock-baronial estate pubs which, due to their ornate style and the scale of the expansion, led to their being known as Tolly Follies. They were based on the design of the Tollemache stately home, Helmingham Hall. The Golden Hind is the least altered of these pubs, and prior to a major refurbishment in 1999 it was virtually as built. Its external features include a clock tower (there is an appeal to restore it into use), 11 ornate chimneys and a large loggia at the rear. There is an identically built pub also called the Golden Hind on Milton Road, Cambridge, but its interior is much changed.

On the right a revolving door leads into a large space where the oak room and the room

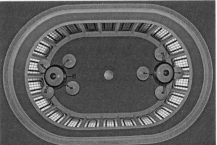

behind were made into one. Above the back section is an imposing, elaborately ornamented, oval-shaped lantern skylight. The original staircase with turned baluster leads to a large function room that retains two original fireplaces. Some of the fine oak panelling from the former oak room survives, but the original bar has been replaced by a new one to the rear. On the left is the L-shaped public bar. Immediately ahead is an ornamentally screened cubicle with leaded lights; this originally shielded the off-sales, though it is now difficult to work out how it was accessed. The bar fittings in this room

are new with only a little panelling near the pool table of historic interest. This is one of few pubs with an Ipswich Fives Dart Board which only appears for matches (see p84).

470 Nacton Road, IP3 9NF · 01473 724025
 ipswichgoldenhind; Listed Grade II; Planning: Ipswich;
Real ale; Meals lunch and evening (not Sun eve).

Taking it Home

Where did you last buy a drink to take home? Chances are it was a super-market, perhaps a convenience store, or maybe a high street drinks shop. It's hardly likely to have been down at your local pub. Up until around 50 years ago, though, it would have been a different story. Many pubs sold drinks of all kinds for customers to enjoy at home, and very often there was special provision in the building's layout to cater for this. Legislation changed in the 1960s to enable super-markets to sell alcohol freely, and the rest is history. The 'offie' at the pub is now largely a thing of the past.

Off-sales areas went under a bewildering variety of names: off-sales (of course), jug and bottle (and vice versa), outdoor department, order department, jug department and so on. You can sometimes still see the old names fossilised in etched glass or doorplates – the left-hand door of the Swan in Bushey (p61), for instance, has 'Jug and Bottle Entrance' etched on it.

Two of our featured pubs have separate off-sales still in use. At the Rose, Shotley, Essex (p113), you'll see, if you enter the left-hand door, another door ahead of you. Behind this is the little offie, known as 'the slip'. Customers use it to buy drinks, sweets and even some toys.

Rose, Shotley

The Rose & Crown, Bury St Edmunds (p100), has an off-sales with its own entrance between the public and saloon bars. The tiny, narrow room, more like a passage, has a tongue-and-groove panelled dado. Three handpumps sit on the old counter, behind which is a part-mirrored bar-back with modern

Rose & Crown, Bury St Edmunds

shelving added to the left. The main use today is to sell confectionery, but the occasional customer still asks for a jug to be filled with real ale – not something you can buy at the supermarket!

Many off-sales, particularly in larger pubs, were accessed by their own external door (or via a door in the lobby) and were tiny rooms with a counter and bar-back shelves. Until quite recently, a fully intact example could be found at the Painters Arms, Luton (p26). The fantastic 'Jug Bar' itself is still there, albeit now used as a tiny snug rather than for its original off-sales purpose. It comprises two three-quarter-height partition walls with Art Nouveau-style glazing at the top and still has the original counter; the seats, now sadly removed, ran down each side and allowed customers to have a swift one before returning home.

Swan, Bushey

Painters Arms, Luton

Taking it Home

Elsewhere, the off-sales is still there but now closed off. At the Margaret Catchpole, Ipswich (p104), for instance, the fully wood-panelled space is as large as some snugs; it has a bar counter and shelved bar-back plus 'retail' in a stained and leaded door-window – but is now used for storage. The same applies at the White Admiral, Harlow (p56).

The reason why off-sales were quite separate from other rooms is that, historically, many pubs were the preserve of men; it was invariably women (and occasionally children) who brought a jug to be filled with beer for working men. Screened-off areas stopped them from seeing the blokes in the bar and vice-versa.

Where there was no special enclosed small space for off-sales, a hatch might be provided facing the front door or in a corridor. The East of England has some good surviving examples, albeit not now used for their original purpose. The Hand & Heart, Peterborough (p40), has a corridor running from the front door, halfway along which is a screen with a tiny, hinged panel that can be opened for off-sales; there's also a bell push to advise staff that a customer is wanting service. More recently, this area has become a modest drinking lobby with a couple

Queen's Head, Newton

of stools. The lower sash screen is raised nowadays.

From the front door of the Queen's Head, Newton, Cambridgeshire (p36), a short passage takes you to a hatch, still with its twin windows, bell push and 'Jug and Bottle' doorplate.

Sometimes, all you can now see is an unused off-sales window – the Angel, Larling, Norfolk (p83), and Jolly Sailor, Orford, Suffolk (p110), are examples.

Angel, Larling

Jolly Sailor, Orford

The former bottle and jug at the Walnut Tree, Broads Green, Essex (p46), is now the delightful snug.

Hand & Heart, Peterborough

Walnut Tree, Broads Green

IPSWICH

Margaret Catchpole ★★★

A very precious survival, and one of few inter-war Grade II*-listed pubs. Built in 1936 by the local Cobbold Brewery, this is the very embodiment of everything that inter-war pub builders were aiming for – refined architecture, restrained, elegant furnishings, and the added bonus of sporting facilities. What's more, it is wholly intact and as such one of only a handful left in the country. The remarkable exterior draws on vernacular traditions with large, sweeping roofs, and prominent dormers and chimney stacks, presenting a varied, asymmetrical façade to the road.

Public bar

The interior consists of three unaltered rooms plus an off-sales compartment. The wall panelling and bar counters are exactly as they were in the 1930s and the stock shelving has only suffered minor alteration to accommodate coolers and other late-20th-century serving needs. As you enter by the main entrance the off-sales faces you. It is intact with panelled walls, parquet floor and a solid bar counter plus a '3' on the inside of the door, but the tiny room is now only used for storage. Turn left into the spacious public bar, the bay window of which overlooks the bowling green. This has a parquet floor, curving counter and an elegant stone fireplace. One small change here – the gents' on the right/saloon side was originally outside and in the mid-1970s a small link was added. Within the servery look for the bell box with 'Public Bar',

Smoke room

'Smoke Room', 'Retail' and 'Saloon' windows situated above the door for staff to the right side of the counter. The bell push in the saloon – the one nearest the counter – still works; the bell rings and a small disc in one of the windows moves from side to side to indicate where service is required (see p115).

The smaller saloon is situated on the right with 'Saloon' in glazing in the door and its own small, quadrant-shaped bar counter. Sadly, nowadays this room is only used for storage. The panelling here is in the fielded style, very common in inter-war pubs, and there is another polished stone fireplace with a coal fire in it.

Saloon

At the rear comes the smoke room, again with a curved counter, plus a bar-back with its original cupboard and drawers and a wood-block floor; a different pattern adorns the panelled walls here. Look for the rare Ipswich Fives Dart Board (see p84) to the right of the servery, which is ready to play. Other features are the bay window, with a bare bench all the way round which overlooks the bowling green, bell-pushes and a polished stone fireplace. The reason for two doors into the smoke room is that one was the door to the outside gents', which is still there and separate from those for the public bar. Note the 'Ladies' Cloakroom' sign on the door to the toilet.

On the left-hand side is a bowling green, added in 1948 and still in use with a club running eight teams (see p94). A lovely verandah at the back outside the smoke room enables people to watch the play.

Cliff Lane, IP3 0PQ · 01473 252450
 The-Margaret-Catchpole-Inn; Listed Grade II*;
Planning: Ipswich; No real ale; No food.

IPSWICH

Woolpack ★

An attractive, four-roomed pub with an 18th-century brick front to an earlier building. Of great interest is the tiny snug at the front, which could originally have been an off-sales. Access is only by its own door, and it has a counter at least 50 years old. The far-right section of the counter is a recent replacement for a door used by staff, but you need to look closely to spot the difference. One of the smallest pub rooms in the East of England, it has tongue-and-groove panelling with a bare bench attached, but the bar-back shelves are modern.

The lounge on the left (originally the 'Public Parlour') has a fine brick fireplace, painted wainscoting, and a counter from (probably) the 1970s. A passage leads to two small rooms on the right, the first one of which was brought into use in more recent times and has since been more than doubled in size.

1 Tuddenham Road, IP4 2SH · 01473 215862
 ipswichwoolpack; Listed Grade II; Planning: Ipswich; Real ale; Meals Mon–Fri breakfast, lunch & evening, all day Sat & Sun.

Lounge

Snug

LAXFIELD

King's Head (Low House) ★★★

A superlative, unspoilt country pub featuring a most remarkable public bar that is unchanged in 150 years. Along with the Cock, in Broom, Bedfordshire (p23), this is one of only six traditional pubs left in the whole of the UK with no bar counter.

The origins of the building lie in the 16th century, and it was extended on the left in the 18th. It is timber-framed and plastered, with the plaster lined to imitate stonework. Its unspoilt nature is a consequence of being run by the Felgate family from 1882 until 1979. Adnams owned the pub from 1904, but in 2018 it was purchased by the Low House Community Interest Company (CIC), a group of regulars who clubbed together to buy the freehold (see p72). Thankfully, they have carefully restored woodwork that had been disfigured by ghastly 'gastro' pastel shades of paint.

The front doorway leads into the settle room, quite a large space with a red-and-black quarry-tiled floor; it was originally the parlour of the house. Nothing has changed in 150 years, the room being dominated by high Victorian settles on three sides and focused on the log fire with a mantelshelf almost reaching the ceiling. Note the trivet for placing a joint of meat on for roasting over the hearth, and cupboards on either side for keeping things warm and dry.

The backs of the settles, with iron stays attached to the ceiling, define a corridor that runs right round the room and has an old, basic bench. There really is nothing quite like this room anywhere else and it is undoubtedly the core of the pub.

On the right, a latch door leads to the card room, which is in the 16th-century part of the building and would have been the kitchen of the house. It has a black-and-red quarry-tiled floor, fixed seats all around the room attached to the old tongue-and-groove dado panelled walls, an old (now disused) wood surround fireplace and just two scrubbed tables. On the long table are markings that relate to a Far Eastern game called 'Go'.

Behind this, the tap room was possibly brought into use at a later date. It contains three-sided pew seating around a large, scrubbed table, plain panelling and a tongue-and-groove and panelled ceiling; opposite this a large, multi-drawered old cupboard is the storage place for crisps and nuts.

Behind this is the servery, which is actually the cellar, with a concrete screeded floor and no counter – but it is here that you come to place your order and have your beer served direct from casks on stillage. As you enter, look on the right for the wooden structure that was an early servery, now with some modern shelves.

At the end of the passage around the settles, through a low doorway and over a small step, is a small lobby with an uneven brick floor leading to the dining room in the rear left-hand part of the pub. This was originally the living room and brought into use in 1992 to meet expanded trade. It has good but modern settle seating and scrubbed tables in keeping with the rest of the pub, and a genuine early-20th-century tiled and cast fireplace.

As befits a pub as unspoilt as this, the toilets are outside.

Closed Mon.   Gorams Mill Lane, IP13 8DW · 01986 798395
 LowHouseLaxfield; Listed Grade II; Planning: Mid Suffolk; Real ale; Meals Tue–Sat lunchtime & evening; also Sun lunchtime.

Card room

Top room

Settle Down in a Snug

Snugs formed using settles were once widespread throughout England but are now relatively rare. Some of the most impressive survivals of the arrangement can be found in the East of England. Most surround a fireplace so were presumably created to protect roaring fires from the draughts caused by front doors opening and closing.

The star among them has to be that at the King's Head, Laxfield, Suffolk (p106). As soon as you open the front door, you'll see the snug, known as the settle room on account of it being dominated by high, wooden settles on the east, south and west sides; the backs of them define a corridor running around the room, a rare, historic arrangement. One settle is parallel to the front wall – one of two sides (south and east) is fixed to the beamed ceiling by way of two curved iron brackets.

The snug at the Red Lion, Kenninghall, Norfolk (p82), is just to the right of the entrance. It clearly started life as a big settle which then had boarding extended to the ceiling and side. Why there's a rectangular hinged opening over the doorway, nobody knows. It's undeniably a delightful place to sup a beer though.

Crown, Snape

with an iron bracket holding it to the ceiling. The cosiness rating of this space is somewhere near the maximum.

Again in windy Suffolk is the Bell, Walberswick (p114), where the snug is similar in style to the King's Head. A small settle is on one side with a long one facing two sides, but the gap between them is greater than at Laxfield. The settles are held in place with five wooden pillars.

Bell, Walberswick

Elsewhere, we can find other snugs that feature settles. The example at the Green Dragon, Wymondham, Norfolk (p92), is at the back of the pub and was even

Green Dragon, Wymondham

more impressive up until 1993 when removal of the central section left a wide gap between the curved part on the left and another settle on the right. Both have a section added, perhaps in the inter-war period, reaching the ceiling and including some latticed, leaded glazed panels.

The Horse & Groom, Hatfield, Hertfordshire (p66), has a flagstone-floored snug with a curved settle on

Red Lion, Kenninghall

Moving back to Suffolk, the snug at the Crown, Snape (p113), is also situated just to the right of the front door. It comprises two curved settles with unusual slanting backs, each

Horse & Groom, Hatfield

Settle Down in a Snug

one side, an old fixed bench attached to the opposite wall and a fine ingle-nook fireplace between. The settle has been moved through 90 degrees at some point. In the Green Dragon, Flaunden, Hertfordshire (p62), a floor to ceiling settle forms a short passage into the snug which is to the right of the front door.

Not featured elsewhere in this book because of its opened-up interior, the Coach & Horses, Tilney St Lawrence, Norfolk, has two settles. One is curved and high-backed with a curved iron bracket to the ceiling, the other is long and also high-backed with a section cut out where

Green Dragon, Flaunden

Chequers, Goldhanger

Coach & Horses, Tilney St Lawrence

there's a window; it is fixed to the beamed ceiling with three curved iron brackets.

Why there are so many examples of settle-dominated snugs in the region is a bit of a mystery. Perhaps it's just that the cold winds blowing in from the Urals make East of England drinkers especially appreciative of cosy, intimate spaces – for which we can all be grateful.

White Horse, Eaton Socon

LONG MELFORD

Bull ★

An inn since 1580, there are two rooms of particular interest. At the rear left the public bar was refitted in the early 1960s and retains its impressive counter with fielded panelling and a large bar-back. The original public bar at the front left is now the lounge and is served by a hatch to the rear of the servery. When the bar is closed a fielded panelled screen covers the hatch, a rare survivor. This two-part room is notable for its deeply moulded oak beams – look out for the carving of a 'Wildman' or 'Woodwose'.

To the right of the flagstone entrance passage is the dining room with more oak beams. All three rooms have superb, old, brick fireplaces – the one in the dining room is especially magnificent, 12-ft wide and spanned by a massive, carved-oak mantle beam.

Hall Street, CO10 9JG · 01787 378494
 Bull.LongMelford; Listed Grade II*; Planning: Babergh; Real ale; Meals lunchtime & evening; Accommodation (25 rooms).

Public bar

Wildman carving in lounge

Fireplace in public bar

ORFORD

Jolly Sailor ★

The sea has long deserted the quayside, but an authentic nautical atmosphere lingers at this 17th-century pub formed from two houses. Steps lead down to a simply furnished but superb main bar with low ceiling, flagstone floor and an aged, scrubbed table. The bar counter is at least 70 years old as the photos in the snug show. The tongue-and-groove panelling and some of the bar-back shelves attached could be of similar date. To the right, past an ancient spiral staircase, is the cracking little snug; one panelled wall looks post-war. The dining room to the left has an impressive fireplace. On the far left, down a short passage, is another room with a brick floor, old brick fireplace and wall cupboards. The rear entrance accesses an off-sales hatch to the back of the bar, but this is no longer in use. Alongside it is the small bare-boarded former 'Chart Room', now an office.

Quay Street, IP12 2NU · 01394 450243
 The-jolly-sailor-orford; Listed Grade II; Planning: East Suffolk; Real ale; Meals all day including breakfast; Accommodation (4 rooms).

Snug

Main bar

PIN MILL

Butt & Oyster ★★

The pub occupies a 17th-century building which was enlarged in the 19th century and again in 1932. The public bar, overlooking the water and with its red floor tiles and high-backed settles, is especially attractive. Its little-changed interior is due to the pub being in the Watts family for 50 years till 1983, then Dick and Brenda Mainwaring took over until 2001. The public bar contains some 17th-century fielded panelling and an early 20th-century brick fireplace. The counter was moved back some 18in in 1988. It is hard to date but may be of inter-war vintage, along with the shelves at the back. It looks like beer is served from the casks on the stillage; however, they are there for show, with the actual casks being in the cellar behind and the beer being dispensed via pipes through the tap.

Across the quarry-tiled corridor, which runs through the building, is the small, bare-wood-floored smoke room: it has a brick fireplace over which is a 17th-century carved panel with naively treated figures and contemporary ornamentation. Also enjoying fine views across the river is the dining room, doubled in size in 1932 but with a section of raised floor from 1997, when the panelling and seating in this area were renewed.

Pin Mill and the pub are also popular with film crews. It appeared in an episode of Lovejoy when they changed the name of the pub to 'The Three Ducks'.

IP9 1JW · 01473 780764
 buttandoyster; Listed Grade II; Planning: Babergh; Real ale; Meals breakfast, lunch & evenings.

RUMBURGH

Buck ★

An excellent example of how to expand a pub's trading area by sympathetically creating new, separate rooms. The Buck was run by Jock and Laura Canham from 1926 until Lara retired in 1981 aged 78. In the Canham's days the only public rooms were the public bar at the front left and the little-used 'Men's Kitchen' behind. The public bar retains its old counter front (new top), old, basic, red-painted bar-back shelves, red-painted partition, bare wall-bench seating attached to tongue-and-groove dado panelled walls, and a brick floor. A wall to the left of the bar was removed in 1982 and the licensee's private room on a slightly lower level converted to a small quarry-tiled area with a new, small counter and wall-bench seating/panelling added to match that in the original part. The games room on the far left was originally a stable/barn.

To the rear the flagstone-floored former men's kitchen had a bar added for the first time in 1982 in the style of the public bar one. A photograph in the pub shows two large settles in this room, which were removed by Adnams before they sold the pub in the 1980s. With its imported settle, genuinely old tongue-and-groove panelling on walls and the low ceiling, bench seating, and large brick fireplace, this small room is full of character. At the rear, the small 'Garden Room' was added in the early 1990s. The dining room on the far right was a store room.

Open Mon–Thu 12–3pm and 5–10.30pm.   Mill Road, IP19 0NT
01986 785257 · 🅕 rumburghbuck; Not listed; Planning: East
Suffolk; Real ale; Real draught cider; Meals lunch & evening.

Public bar

Former Men's Kitchen

Public bar

Public bar

SHOTLEY

Rose ★

A delightful, no-nonsense village local where much survives from a 1960s makeover. Ahead of the left-hand door is a further door behind which is an off-sales, known as 'the slip', and which is still in regular use selling drinks, sweets and even some toys (see p102). The public bar on the right has a sloping, 1960s ply-panelled counter with a Formica top and shelving of the same vintage behind. The lounge is accessed from the right-hand door and passage. The counter is also from the 1960s scheme, but has a new top and plain frontage – the bar-back has not been changed. Around 2014 the room was extended to nearly three times its size.

The Street (B1456), IP9 1NL · 01473 787237
 shotleyrose; Not listed; Planning: Bambergh; Real ale; Meals lunch & evening (not Mon lunch).

Public bar

SNAPE

Crown ★★

This 17th-century pub is well worth a visit to see the wonderful snug created by two large, curved settles around a large, old, brick fireplace, all of which could be as much as 200 years old. The settles are held in place by iron stays attached to the beamed ceiling. We are only aware of 15 similar snugs in the country, eight of which are in the East of England (see p108). An uneven, brick floor passageway runs from the front door and to the left is a room with a herringbone brick floor. Situated beyond the snug, the modern bar fittings include a bar-back with linen-fold panelling from the Dorchester in London. This was installed in a refit in the 1990s and involved moving the bar counter through 90 degrees. The bar has since been moved again following flooding in Winter 2013.

Closed Mon, closes at 4pm on Tue, 6pm on Sun.
Bridge Road, IP17 1SL · 01728 689112 · thecrownatsnape; Listed Grade II; Planning: East Suffolk; Real ale; Meals lunch & evening Tue–Sun (not Tue, Sun eve); Accommodation (2 rooms); Camper vans welcome overnight.

SOUTHWOLD

Crown Hotel ★

An 18th-century building with an early Georgian front and impressive inn sign. Included here for the cosy 'Back Bar', nicknamed 'God's Waiting Room'. Situated off the rear tiled corridor, this small room is formed by a curved, glazed partition wall to which bar-back fittings are attached. A section of the glazing operates as a rarely seen hatch with its window intact. The dado panelled walls with plain wood above and bar counter suggest that this room was last refitted in the 1930s. The wall benches are no doubt also pretty old, though now covered with red leatherette. It is good to see that such a traditional bar has been left intact in an otherwise modernised hotel.

High Street, IP18 6DP · 01502 722275
CrownSouthwold; Listed Grade II; Planning: East Suffolk;
Real ale; Meals breakfast, lunch & evening; Accommodation
(14 rooms).

WALBERSWICK

Bell ★

The highlight of this characterful 17th-century village pub is the room at the front left with its uneven flagstone floor, superb, curved L-shaped high-backed settle and smaller settle in front of the old brick fireplace forming a snug. The window bench seating is also old. The front right quarry-tiled room has another old brick fireplace with copper hood and old window bench seating. Originally it was accessed via a door on the right as you enter the pub. The bar counter dates only from 1996. Two tiny rooms can be found off the passage around the settles – the one at the front was an office in the 1930s, while the one at the rear on a lower level was originally the cellar. A modern bar is at the rear with a new dining room on the far left. You can reach the pub from Southwold Harbour by using one of the few remaining hand-operated ferry services; it operates daily in summer and at weekends in the low season.

Ferry Road, IP18 6TN · 01502 723109
BellWalberswick; Listed Grade II; Planning: East Suffolk;
Real ale; Meals lunch & evening; Accommodation (6 rooms).

Snug

Front right room

Table Service

In some old pubs you will find bell pushes dotted round a room. Hardly any of these still work but they are a reminder of a largely forgotten practice – table service. The bells connected to a box in, or visible from, the servery where a bell would ring and an indicator wobble to show where a customer was in need of a drink.

Margaret Catchpole, Ipswich

The only surviving bell box we know of is at the Margaret Catchpole, Ipswich (p104), but it's a belter. It is situated above the staff door to the right of the counter and has 'windows' denoting 'Public Bar', 'Smoke Room', 'Retail' (i.e. off-sales) and 'Saloon'. One of the bell pushes in the saloon still works so, if pushed, a disc in the window moves from side to side. However, the bell is no longer responded to!

In the past, a member of the servery staff or a dedicated waiter would go and take the order, then deliver it. Needless to say, prices in these rooms were a touch higher than in the public bar, and a copper or two by way of a tip to the server was customary. The system worked very efficiently in busy pubs as the waiting staff usually went to a dedicated area of the counter from which other customers were

Maids Head, Norwich

excluded so that they didn't have to fight their way through a crowd of stand-up drinkers.

The Maids Heads, Norwich (p87), offers two examples of bell pushes – several in the inter-war panelled function room and some older-looking ones in the lovely snug. There are two bell pushes at the Red Lion Hotel, Cromer (p78), an ornate one and another alongside a fireplace now has a sign that tells you not to push it!

Red Lion Hotel, Cromer

The wonderful front settle area at the King's Head, Laxfield, Suffolk (p106), wouldn't seem complete without an old-fashioned bell and sure enough there is one.

King's Head, Laxfield

Elsewhere in the country, the traditional form of table service survives in only a handful of pubs. However, the recent pandemic saw table service imposed on pubs for a while and some operators, notably J D Wetherspoon, continue to encourage its use. You can order drinks and food from the comfort of your seat, albeit using an app on your phone rather than pushing a bell – and it won't cost you a penny more.

Maids Head, Norwich

Danger Do Not Touch
Red Lion Hotel, Cromer

Heritage Pubs of the Future?

The main listings in this book feature pubs that are largely unchanged in the last 50 years – but during that period many pubs have been restored and others created in buildings previously used for something else. CAMRA is recording the best quality examples of such pubs, some of which will no doubt become the heritage pubs of the future, and we recommend the following East of England pubs as being well worth a visit. Most have stunning interiors of significant architectural merit; some faithfully achieve a genuinely historic look and feel.

CAMBRIDGESHIRE

Free Press, Prospect Row, Cambridge, CB1 1DU

This pub closed in 1976 when the whole area was slated for redevelopment, but, happily, the planners had a change of heart and sold it back to Greene King who reopened it in 1978. What you see now is largely a faithful reproduction of what was, and still is, a characterful, traditional back-street pub. The main changes are loss of a partition that created the off-sales and the

Free Press, Cambridge, snug

amalgamation of the small right-hand bar with a former private sitting room. Fittings like the bar counter, bar-back, dado panelling and fireplaces replicate the originals. The tiny, partitioned snug, measuring 6ft by 5ft, is, however, totally original. Not listed.

Free Press, Cambridge, bar and snug

Hippodrome, Dartford Road, March, PE15 8AQ

Originally a cinema from 1928, the building became a bingo hall in 1970 before being partly reopened as a cinema once more between 2001 and 2009. Wetherspoons then stepped in and, after a major and very careful refurbishment, it opened as a pub in 2011. Many original Art Deco features survive, including the circle, moulded box fronts, a 32-ft wide proscenium arch and a 24-ft deep stage. Not listed.

Wortley Almshouses, Westgate, Peterborough, PE1 1QA

Built as almshouses in 1837, this was converted to a one-roomed pub in 1981, its Grade II listing having saved it from demolition as part of the adjacent Queensgate development. In 2003 Samuel Smiths brewery reconfigured the interior into six small rooms, a layout more akin to the style of the original almshouses; this work won the Best Pub Refurbishment category in the CAMRA Pub Design Awards 2003.

ESSEX

Compasses, Littley Green, CM3 1BU

The brewery tap of Ridleys Brewery, which was sold to Greene King and closed in 2005. Ridleys had carried out an excellent renovation here around 1990, creating the present layout by bringing a former private room into public use. The three rooms, with their tiled floors, wood-panelled walls and bare bench seating, all look entirely authentic. The public bar has an open fire and basic bar-back shelving. Real ales and cider are drawn direct from the cellar and food includes giant baps called Huffers. Not listed.

Playhouse, St John's Street, Colchester, CO2 7AA

Opened as a theatre in 1929, the building was redesigned as a cinema in 1935 with the gallery removed and balcony enlarged; there were seats for 1,158 patrons. From 1981 to 1993 it was a Bingo Club. Wetherspoons then restored it with their customary attention to detail and it reopened in 1994. The stage has been kept and is decorated with a set as if for a play. Up in the balcony, life-sized models of famous people occupy the seats. Not listed.

Playhouse, Colchester

HERTFORDSHIRE

Old Cross Tavern, St Andrew Street, Hertford, SG14 1JA

The pub occupies a late-17th-century Grade II-listed building, converted from an antiques shop in 1999. The interior is essentially a single room with some screened-off small areas. The ambience and service (no TV or music, just good, old-fashioned conversation) fully live up to their slogan of 'Pubs the Way they Used to be'. A range of real ales is offered, sometimes from the pub's own microbrewery. Opens at 4.30pm Mon–Thu, 4pm on Fri, 2pm Sat–Sun.

Waterend Barn, Civic Close, St Albans, AL1 3LE

A 17th-century barn was moved from Wheathampstead to the city centre in 1939 for use as a restaurant. In 1964, it was joined by a Grade II-listed 16th-century barn from Little Hormead near Buntingford. The building was acquired by Wetherspoons in 2004 and they have done a typically good job of integrating pub use into the spaces, creating four drinking areas, and highlighting the half-timbered walls and exposed roof timbers.

NORFOLK

Lattice House, Chapel Street, King's Lynn, PE30 1EG

This timber-framed, Grade II*-listed merchant's house dates from around 1480 and is therefore the oldest building featured in this book, along with the Green Dragon, Wymondham (p92). It became a pub in 1980 and was bought by Wetherspoons in 2000. They subsequently sold it and it reopened under new ownership

in October 2019. The interior has many rooms, spread over two floors, and retains many interesting old features, notably the impressively high-beamed roof, minstrels' gallery and large inglenook fireplace.

Cosy Club, London Street, Norwich, NR2 1HX

Completed as the National Provincial Bank in 1925 and closed as a bank in 2017, this ornate, Grade II-listed building has been sensitively restored, making the most of its Art Deco features. The huge, domed ceiling in what was the banking hall is truly awe-inspiring. The old vault has been turned into a private dining room. No real ale.

Gunton Arms, Cromer Road, Thorpe Market, NR11 8TZ

This started life in Victorian times as the shooting lodge for Gunton Hall, hence its situation in the 1,000-acre deer park surrounding the Hall. During the 1890s a frequent visitor was Lillie Langtry, actress, famous beauty, and mistress of the future King Edward VII. Later becoming a hotel, it was bought in 2011 by an art dealer and his artist wife who oversaw a detailed restoration programme which has radically transformed the interior. The many different rooms and spaces all ooze character and are enhanced by many artworks from the owners' own collection. A true visual treat as well as an excellent pub/restaurant/hotel. Grade II listed.

Three Horseshoes,
Bridge Street, Warham All Saints, NR23 1NL

The pub originally occupied just the block bearing the pub sign and, until the 1960s, comprised the current bar plus a snug, now the servery. This room has a quarry-tiled floor,

dado panelling and scrubbed benches. Note the Norfolk twister game (see p38) hanging from the ceiling. The cupboards in the servery are genuinely old but the shelving is relatively recent. In 1982 a hole was cut in the wall between the bar and the former snug to create the small hatch/counter. The other two rooms look authentically old but are later creations – one was formerly a general store. Not listed.

SUFFOLK

Corn Exchange, Abbeygate Street, Bury St Edmunds, IP33 1UL
Built in 1861/2 and originally a provisions market, the Corn Exchange was proposed for demolition in the 1960s to be replaced by shops. Eventually, a compromise was reached to save the building by inserting a new first floor. The Grade II-listed building is now a multi-purpose venue, with the first floor opening as a Wetherspoons pub in 2012. Being so close to the grand, arched, glass roof, with its decorated central plaster panel, you can walk through the

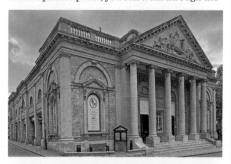

semi-circular stone arches, admiring the ornate keystones which display agricultural motifs like wheatsheaves and rams' heads. The overall effect is stunning.

Isaacs on the Quay, Wherry Way, Ipswich, IP4 1AS
This was once the maltings for the nearby Tolly Cobbold brewery, who later developed it as a pub called the Malt Kiln. It then became a wine and vodka bar before being greatly extended in 2009. Under its new ownership, it occupies an enviable quayside location and offers a wide variety of drinking spaces on different levels, all smartly kitted out in contemporary style. Most of the Grade II*-listed building itself dates from the late-18th/early-19th-century, though some parts are older.

St Peter's Hall, St Peter South Elmham, Bungay, NR35 1NQ
A Grade-II* listed 15th-, 16th- & 17th-century former manor house complete with moat. The ecclesiastical windows and the porch are from Flixton Priory, a monastic establishment dissolved by Cardinal Wolsey in the 1520s. It was converted to a pub in 1996 by the adjacent St Peter's brewery, who have different opening hours for brewery tours and the shop. St Peter's Hall consists of the high-ceilinged Great Hall which has a fine, carved, wooden screen, a large Brussels tapestry depicting Manna from heaven,

St Peter's Hall, St Peter South Elmham

billiards, a piano and the only game of 'Ring the Hartebeest' in the country, using a hartebeest horn from South Africa. In the small lounge are a wood-burning stove, a high-backed settle, pew seating and a large, scrubbed table. Opens 7pm Fri–Mon plus Sun lunchtime. Not listed.

and a huge, Tudor-style stone and brick fireplace. The smaller room houses the bar and has an old fireplace with a bread oven. There are further rooms on the first floor including a small chapel. Prior to a visit, check the Trio Catering website www.trioscatering.co.uk/trios-restaurant – St Peter's Hall is closed Mon to Wed and has limited opening hours on other days.

White Horse, Low Road, Sweffling, IP17 2BB

A characterful 'de-modernisation' that could fool the unwary into believing it is genuinely ancient. This cosy, two-roomed pub has no bar counter, the beer being stillaged in a small alcove in the tap room. The public bar has a red quarry-tiled floor, a large cooking range, bar

The Outstanding Conversions and Restorations Project

CAMRA's national project to identify pubs such as these is called 'Outstanding Conversions & Restorations'. You can find full details of the project, including the pub listings, at https://ocrpubs.camra.org.uk

When assessing pubs, surveyors are primarily looking for examples of outstanding **quality**. This can derive either directly from the previous incarnation of the building, or from the way the interior has been adapted and designed, or both. The aims of the initiative are two-fold:

– to raise awareness and enjoyment of the best recent pub design;

– to inspire pub owners and others to pursue excellence when converting or restoring buildings for pub use.

Glossary

Ale: originally a fermented malt liquor, made without the use of hops. The term has been effectively interchangeable with 'beer' for at least the last 200 years.

Alehouse/beerhouse: originally a house selling ale/beer, but not wine or spirits. Their numbers expanded greatly after the 1830 Beer Act under which any ratepayer could open such an establishment on payment of two guineas for a licence. Numbers reduced as magistrates regained control with the 1869 and 1872 Licensing Acts. Today there is no separate licensing category, so the institution has formally disappeared.

Art Deco: a fashionable style between the two world wars in Europe and America. It relies on geometrical patterns and sleek lines. The name comes from the Exposition International des Arts-Décoratifs in Paris in 1924–5 which greatly enhanced its popularity.

Art Nouveau: a style reliant on flowing lines and sinuous forms, often based on nature and the human form. It was popular from about 1890 until 1914, though more so in Europe than the UK. Sometimes makes an appearance in pub tiles and windows.

Baffle: a wooden screen, often at the end of bench seating, placed near a door to help keep out draughts.

Balustrade: row of small posts or columns lining a staircase or raised area, topped with a rail.

Bar-back: shelving, sometimes very ornately treated and incorporating mirrors, at the rear of a servery.

Barrel: although widely used as a term for any size of cask, the term applies, strictly speaking, to a vessel containing 36 gallons. This used to be the standard size for beer casks until the mid-20th century. Today, the standard cask contains nine gallons and is properly termed a firkin.

Barrel ceiling: a ceiling with one or more curved sections, like the inside of half a barrel.

Bell push: a button that activated an electric bell or a visual indicator when there was table service in the better-class rooms of many pubs.

Big Six: the dominant group of major breweries which emerged in the 1960s, controlling 56% of all pubs by 1972 (as against 24% in 1960). They were: Allied, Bass Charrington, Courage, Watneys (Grand Metropolitan), Scottish & Newcastle and Whitbread. By 1972 they were brewing 92% of the UK's beer.

Bottle and jug: see off-sales.

Brewers' Tudor: a style, especially popular between the world wars, which drew nostalgically upon the half-timbered architecture of the Tudor period. Within pubs, it was often associated with fully panelled rooms.

Canted: sloping – as seen in some bar counters.

Carrstone: a sandstone conglomerate that varies in colour from light to dark, rusty ginger.

Cellar: a room where casks are stored, usually, but not necessarily, below ground.

Coaching inn: strictly, an inn on one of the main coaching routes, where horses would be changed and where passengers could obtain refreshment. Today, the term is applied indiscriminately to any inn, whether or not it was a calling-place for coaches.

Cornice: a strip of plaster, wood or stone going along the top of a wall where it meets the ceiling.

Dado: the lower part of a wall, often but not always below a rail and above a skirting board and also often wood panelled.

Draught screen: see Baffle.

Fielded panelling: a series of wooden panels with a raised or recessed square or rectangular central section, usually found in wall panelling or bar counter fronts.

Formica: a laminate product, very popular in the 1950s and 1960s for counter tops or other surfaces needing to be kept clean.

Free house: a pub not tied to a brewer, whose landlord is free to obtain beer from any source. The term is abused by most modern pub companies, who do not brew themselves but insist that their tenants obtain beer from specified suppliers.

Frieze: a broad, horizontal band of sculpted or painted decoration, usually on a wall near the ceiling.

Gable: the portion of a wall, usually triangular, between the edges of intersecting roof pitches.

Gastropub: a late-20th-century term for a pub where the main emphasis is on food.

Gravity dispense: beer or cider served direct from the cask into the glass.

Half-timbering: see Brewers' Tudor.

Hall house: an early house design dominated by an open, often large, central hall

Handpump: the lever on the bar which operates a beer engine to draw beer from the cask in the cellar, and now universally regarded as the standard method of dispense for real ale (q.v.).

Hatch: an opening to a servery from an adjoining room, sometimes with a small shelf and/or a window.

Herringbone: an arrangement of rectangular blocks used in flooring whose pattern resembles the bones of a fish such as a herring.

Hogshead: a cask containing 54 gallons.

Improved public houses: built between the wars with the aim of making the pub respectable. They tended to be large, had a wide range of facilities, and sought to attract a 'better' class of customer.

Inglenook: a recess, often substantial, adjoining a fireplace, and sometimes with seating at both extremities.

Inn: originally a house offering accommodation and refreshment to travellers. More recently, the term has been loosely applied to any kind of pub establishment.

Jug and bottle: see off-sales.

Lapped wood: planks or boards which overlap each other.

Linen-fold: a simple style of relief carving used to decorate wood panelling, and which resembles folded linen.

Loggia: an outdoor corridor or gallery, roofed but otherwise open to the elements.

Lounge (bar): originally the most comfortably furnished (and 'better class') room in a public house. Beer was usually more expensive in the lounge bar.

Mock Baronial: a popular Victorian architectural style that harked back to the fortified domestic buildings of the Middle Ages.

Mock-Tudor: see Brewers' Tudor.

Moderne: a fairly modest, sleek and somewhat simplified version of Art Deco (q.v.). It featured curving forms and smooth, polished surfaces.

Naively treated: produced in an unsophisticated, direct (but often attractive) style.

Norfolk Pammets: sometimes 'pamments', these terracotta floor tiles are made from materials local to Norfolk.

Off-sales: sales of drink for consumption off the premises. The term is sometimes applied to the place in the pub where the sales take place (which also goes by other names such as jug and bottle).

Pammet: see Norfolk Pammets.

Parquet: geometric mosaic of wood pieces used for decorative effect in flooring.

Partition: basically, something that divides a space, usually non-load-bearing walls or wooden screens.

Pediment: a triangular or sometimes curved structure built over a door or window as a decoration.

Portico: external colonnaded porch or entrance to a building.

Pot-shelf: a shelf or structure over a bar counter for housing glasses. They are a late-20th-century development, and have profoundly and often adversely affected the appearance of many pubs.

Private bar: a somewhat more select area than the public bar. The name implies occupancy by a group of regulars known to one another.

Pubco: a pub-owning company with no brewing interests. They arose out of the Beer Orders of 1989.

Public bar: the most basic pub room (known sometimes simply as the bar) where drink was slightly cheaper than in the better rooms.

Quarry tile: plain, unglazed floor tiles, usually red and black, often laid in square or lozenge patterns and popular for pub flooring.

Real ale: a term coined in the early 1970s to describe traditional beer, which undergoes a secondary fermentation and conditioning in the barrel (hence the alternative term 'cask-conditioned' as opposed to 'keg' beers, which are brewery-conditioned).

Rendering: the process of covering a wall with cement, lime or some other mixture. Popular for pub exteriors.

Saloon: a better-class pub room.

Screeded floor: one comprised of concrete that has been levelled and flattened before finishing.

Servery: the area, almost always behind a bar-counter, from which drinks are dispensed.

Settle: bench-seating, often curved, with a medium to high back.

Slatted: narrow, overlapping strips of wood.

Smoke room: a better-class pub room. In former times, when smoking was not a social issue, there is no reason to suppose that smoking was restricted to this area. It is likely that, being better furnished than the public bar, the room was somehow associated with taking one's ease, as in the smoking room of country houses.

Snug: a small, intimate room.

Spittoon: a receptacle (or trough) for spit but no doubt accumulating cigar and cigarette ends, ash and other small refuse. Both spit and sawdust were commonplace in the public bar, giving rise to a phrase to describe a basic establishment or room.

Stillage: a framework on which casks are mounted or 'stillaged' ready for service. The name may have arisen from the need for traditional beer to remain still for a period to allow it to clear before service.

Tap room: a pub room of similar status to the public bar. Puzzlingly, despite what the name might suggest, drink was rarely dispensed from within them as they tended to be separate from the servery.

Tavern: originally an urban drinking house serving expensive imported wine, as well as good-quality food, to better-off customers. In modern times, the term has been adopted by all kinds of pub establishment.

Teetotal: abstaining from all alcoholic drink.

Temperance: advocacy of drinking little or no alcohol. The earliest campaigners, around 1830, promoted moderation and only boycotted spirits. Later on, increasing numbers became teetotal. (See article on p77.)

Terracotta: (literally, fired earth) very hard-wearing, unglazed pottery.

Terrazzo: flooring consisting of small pieces of marble set in concrete, rubbed down and polished.

Tied house: a public house which is committed to taking a particular brewery's beers, either because it is owned or leased by that brewery, or because the owner has accepted a loan in exchange for selling those beers alone (the so-called 'loan-tie').

Tongue(d)-and-groove(d) boarding: in pubs, cheap panelling on walls and ceilings and consisting of boards with tongues cut along one edge and grooves in the opposite edge, which are then joined together.

Vaulted ceiling: a ceiling made up of self-supporting arched forms, usually of stone or brick.

Vestibule: a small space between an entrance and the main interior of a building.

Victorian-style fireplace: a fairly recently installed fireplace, designed in a Victorian style, usually with cast-iron grate and tiled and wood surround. Genuine Victorian fireplaces are very rare.

Wainscotting: see Dado

Wattle and Daub: a wall building method in which wooden strips ('wattles') are daubed with a sticky material normally made from combining wet soil, clay, sand, straw and animal dung.

Index

Page numbers in **bold** indicate illustrations